Contents

INTRODUCTION

It is often said of the courts that all human life is there. In the decade 1970—1980 that I spent in and around the court rooms of the Republic of Ireland, as a journalist with the *Irish Times,* I saw an astonishing parade come to answer the rule of law. Babies were held in arms in the Children's Court as the Justice decided where they should go; Cabinet Ministers appeared in the dock; eight year olds who played football in the streets were brought in by guards and convicted; businessmen who assaulted each other in discotheques brought charges and countercharges; a mother of thirteen children who stole trousers for her unemployed husband received a suspended sentence.

Religion, sex and politics had a high profile. Members of the Hare Krishna movement were summonsed for walking in the streets; the Maoists were convicted of postering and sent to jail for contempt; homosexuals were convicted; the State loitered in prosecuting a man charged with buggery and he was released to molest two children before final conviction.

Entire and decimated and estranged families appeared in the dock, and neighbours besides. Husbands beat up their wives; avoided paying maintenance to their wives; were occasionally assaulted by their wives. Parents summonsed their children; in-laws became out-laws after conviction.

Neighbours accused each other; friends assaulted each other; some appeared surprised, and accused, together, after a night on the tiles. Winos and beggars were hauled in; demented women, vague men, wandering children trooped regularly through.

There was real crime too — burglary, theft, forgery, stealing cars, all too often committed by men who began their careers in childrens' reformatories and were processed through St. Patrick's, Mountjoy, Dundrum Mental Hospital, and back to Mountjoy again, with occasional breaks in the fresh air and no hope of a life outside institutional walls.

The travelling people are regularly fined in pounds shillings and pence and released back to the bridges where they begged them; often they go to jail.

People are found innocent of charges originally brought against them, and then convicted of having resisted the guards in the course of arrest; or obstructing them, or assaulting them. A prison sentence is often imposed.

In the midst of this bedlam, whilst waiting for the law to take its course, people apply for bail and freedom. The relatives who come to buy them out are refused — the father is not earning enough, the mother is earning nothing, the Credit Union book is rejected. Banks are thicker than blood.

The law is subject to the season of the year — around Christmas, the Justice promises jail for shoplifters — and often dependent on the personality of the Justice. One likes to jail drug addicts, another likes to put them under probation.

In the ten years that I spent in and around the courts, I learned that there is a clear distinction between law and justice. The parent who steals for food for the children is praised in parable and convicted in the court; the alcoholic who needs treatment is punished; the beggar who needs money is jailed; the person who goes to jail again and again, and is not rehabilitated, is sent back to the jail again and again and again.

Because these people have suffered more than enough by appearing in court in the first place, I never used their real names and addresses. I have named the Justices who decided their fate. Hopefully, this collection of articles will put them in the dock for a change.

A change in the District Courts of this country is urgently needed.

Nell Mc Cafferty
June 1980

Chapter 1
The Majesty of the Law

The gowns and wigs may imply majesty, though they, too, are faded and torn sometimes. The Dublin District Courts themselves have trappings of sadness. As you enter the courtyard, picking your way through cars parked on the sidewalk, there are boys and girls, men and women shouting up to their relatives who push hands and noses, like monkeys, through the Bridewell bars. "Bail," they shout, or "lawyer," or "six months." Often you can't understand and you gesticulate smilingly yourself, like a treed monkey.

In the hallways people stand smoking. There are no ashtrays, nor benches to sit on. Children sit on the steps. Solicitors consult clients as best they can, in the rain or the dirt or the babble. Others, with no money, look hopelessly on. Women wander ignorantly in tears. Men curse, but softly because you can be had up for your anger.

In the yard, away over in the corner, there is a concrete stall to serve as a toilet. Stained lavatory bowls, no lights, no locks, maybe a little paper. No towels, no soap, no mirror.

Within the court itself, no room. Three hard benches, and the unlucky ones line the walls. It gets too hot, too cold, too stuffy, too noisy, too quiet. Even the gardai don't know how to use the microphones. The Justice is irritated. Justice is flawed. The solicitor arrives late. Justice is delayed. The lists are long and the bailsmen have to come back next day. People don't know what to do and other people are too busy to help them. Tempers flare, spirits flag, and the long hopeless grind grinds on.

Around in the High Court, planning permission is debated in leisure and the dignity befitting high finance.

At 4.20 p.m. District Justice Ó hUadhaigh rose abruptly and left the court. Would he come back? The court clerk didn't know. The court sergeant didn't know. The State solicitor didn't know. Nobody knew and three groups of relatives waited to bail out their kin. The sergeant disappeared, the State solicitor wandered off eventually, the court clerk told them that yes, he thought the Justice had gone. But what about bail? Ask at the bail office. They asked at the bail-office. "Ask in the court." The court's closed. Ask somebody, then. They didn't know who to ask.

They stood outside. A woman burst into enraged tears. "How can I get him out?" she grabbed me. I didn't know. "I took the day off work, I'll have to take another day off tomorrow. I can't afford it. For God's sake tell me what to do." I couldn't tell her what to do. A young girl grabbed me. "I had to get me mother to look after the childer. I can't come back to-morrow. My mother is angry enough with him being inside. What'll I do for money? Did you see him telling that woman she didn't own anything? If he owns it, and he's inside, how'll I get him out? What in the name of God will I do?" I didn't know. We stopped a sergeant. He didn't know, and he had to finish his writing. Maybe she knew a priest? he asked her, and she nearly convulsed.

We stopped a solicitor and he suggested going to the other court and trying the Justice there. The solicitor was in a hurry.

District Court 6 was crowded and Justice Good was on the bench. I told the women to let the court sergeant know they wanted bail, and they were frightened. You can't interrupt the sergeant, they said. And you'd have to walk up in front of everybody, and the Justice might be annoyed at the interruption. So they waited.

The Justice ploughed through the cases. They watched the clock and wondered if they'd have time for visiting

4

in the Bridewell. But if they went over there, they might miss the chance to go bail. So they waited, while their husbands and sons reached hands out through the bars. The court finished at quarter to six, and they went up to the sergeant. Too late, he told them, the bails office was closed and he wouldn't be able to get the charge sheets. Too late for the Bridewell too. The prisoners had gone to Mountjoy. The women cried on the pavements outside. Another day off work. Would the boss let her off again? And now they were even late for the children's tea. Would the mother let her out again tomorrow? She was in for a row this night she said. Would her husband understand? I didn't know.

There were problems for Justice Ua Donnchadha too. Two children of the travelling people were up before him and the gardai opposed bail. But where to put them? The nuns, when contacted by phone at the industrial school, had said they "would not have any more." To put them in jail, the Justice would need written or oral evidence that they were "unruly persons." The nuns were not about to come to court and make such uncharitable statements. The Justice had nowhere to put them. The garda reluctantly released them on their own bail. They, at least, got home that night.

16 May 1973

Trapped behind bars

The Guard was clearing people out of the courtyard. "Come on, now," he said, "get out of here. If you've no business in court, you've no business here. The court is finished. Get out of here, come on now." He herded the public like sheep in front of him, his arms outstretched, waggling his hands. It was actually a quarter past three, and though the Justices had risen, awaiting further business, the courts do not close until four o'clock. But the guard said so, and they moved resentfully away, calling to relatives behind bars, up in the Bridewell cells.

A woman with two children, one of them in a pram, stopped me and asked me to help. She was crying. A

5

young man stopped alongside her and asked me to help. He was bewildered. His brother had just been ordered into custody for a week, and he wanted to see him before they took him to Mountjoy. He wanted to know what the charges were, and if he could help. The guard in charge of the Bridewell had not been helpful.

We stopped a Garda inspector, who was in a hurry. Ask the man at the desk, he said. It was the business of the man at the desk. We went into the Bridewell and asked the man at the desk. He was irascible and short-tempered and brusque. No visits allowed, he said shortly. That was that. No visits. Too many prisoners. No time. We persisted, quietly. Visits had been allowed in other cases, we said. That was at his discretion, said the man behind the desk. No discretion today. Go to Mountjoy tomorrow. We pleaded, like underlings, for a little discretion. No, said the man behind the desk. The brother walked disconsolately away. You can't argue with a guard, he said. His brother was locked in. He was locked out. The guards and the courts and the State between them.

The woman in the courtyard was hiding with her children behind the parked cars. I called her out. We could talk in the street, she said, looking around for the guard who put people out of the courtyard. We could talk here, I assured her. She was crying.

"My husband can't get bail. He's in jail. The case has been going on for months, and they sent him for trial last Friday. They said he needed a new bail. His father went up for him for months. The inspector always said it was all right, because the father has a good job. But the inspector wasn't there when the father was, and the Justice refused him. It's the same Justice who always accepted him before. But the father has no money in the bank and he was refused.

"I've been here since Friday trying to get him bail. The Justice refused another man today, and my husband's going for an interview with C.I.E. on Thursday, and he's been out of work for six months, I have to get him out."

The bail was for two independent sureties of £100 or one of £200. An aunt had gone bail for £100 yesterday.

"We were in court all day. It takes up a lot of your time. All day Friday here with the children. All day Monday, and the aunt lost a day's pay. All day today.

"A man went bail today, but he had a previous conviction, and the Justice refused it. I've tried everybody and I can't get him out. What will I do? For God's sake what will I do? I've been here since Friday."

Did she not know anyone with a car, or a stereo set, or money in the post office, or with their own house, I asked her. Only on her own side of the family, she said, and they didn't talk to her any more. "I told people about it, people I know, but they didn't make any comment on the bail, so I knew not to ask them. They were embarrassed. So was I. They think if you appear in the court, you must be in trouble, and they don't want anything to do with it."

Was she worth nothing herself, I asked. It was the first time she smiled. No, nothing. Only bits of furniture. Did she know any priests, I asked. She knew the parish priest vaguely. Could you ask a priest, she wondered. She didn't know him too well.

Then she burst out again. Why had the father been refused? Her husband had always turned up for the case. Was there no way she could get him out? Did you have to be worth money? He was unemployed, and who is worth money apart from businessmen? She didn't know any businessmen.

She was tired and hungry. She walked away, pushing the pram, holding the other child by the hand. She had been in the court every day, so she didn't have time to visit him in Mountjoy. She couldn't take the time to go there, because she had to get bail for him to get him out for the interview on Thursday.

She stopped at the gate. The trial mightn't come for weeks. Would they hold him all that time? Was there no way she could get him out? Did you have to be worth money, she asked again. Sure who would have a hundred pounds? She walked away off then.

In court two weeks ago, a District Justice asked a businessman who offered himself in substantial bail if he was in credit with the bank. "No," said the business-

7

man. The Justice burst into laughter. "I haven't been in credit myself since the day I was married," he said, and he accepted the businessman. Then he asked me not to pay attention to what he said. Since he asked, I will not give the Justice's name. But if neither he nor businessmen can be expected to be in credit, isn't it a rather harsh requirement to demand of the working class? Just because, like the Justice, a family could not furnish evidence of £100 in credit a man is in prison, and his family is suffering.

27 February 1976

The worth of women

"Are you worth £80?", the justice asked the father who wanted to go bail for his son. The man smiled and looked at him, then at the court clerk, then back to the justice.

"What?", he asked. "Are you worth £80", the justice asked again, more loudly, sitting forward in his high chair. The man smiled again, politely, and fingered his ear.

"Look are you worth £80?" Justice Ó hUadhaigh snarled into the microphone, his voice amplifying, as the clerk leapt from his chair and spoke directly into the man's ear.

The man listened to the clerk, who turned round and told the justice then that the man was deaf. "Ah, I'm sorry, I'm sorry," the justice said, and the man said he hadn't got £80.

"Refused" the Justice said, adding as the man left the witness box, "You didn't indicate you were deaf. Though you seemed quite well up to that".

Another application for bail was granted to a man who offered his cameras as security, and the court rose for a while.

The deaf man had rejoined his wife and daughter on the benches. They were agitated, and they went forward to the policeman in charge and spoke to him. I did explain your rights to you, he said, there's nothing more I can do.

"I thought he meant had I £80 on me", the man said

to me. "We don't know what's going on", his wife said. We don't know what you're supposed to do here. We've furniture worth hundreds, would that not do". I explained to her that household goods are not accepted. Should the defendant not turn up for his next appearance, the court would not take away a person's furniture. That would be submitting the family to hardship. They'd take your house as security, though (there's no hardship in estreating a house).

They didn't own their house. They didn't have a car. The daughter said she could go bail. Her husband had money in the savings. He had a good job, a soldier in the army. He couldn't come himself as he was on duty far from Dublin. She would offer herself.

She was her husband's dependant, I explained to her. She had to be worth something in her own right. She realised she was technically worth nothing in her own right. The mother then said she would go bail. She had her credit union book. Had she savings, I asked her. Oh yes. The policeman took her out to the corridor, to go to an office.

The justice was recalled and the woman was sworn in, polite and eager and smiling.

"Are you worth £80 over and above your just and lawful debts?" Justice Ó hUadhaigh asked her.

"Oh, yes," she assured him, smiling, "I have my credit union book here". She fumbled for it in her bag, couldn't find it.

"Take your time, ma'am", Justice Ó hUadhaigh said to her, with a smile. She smiled back, fumbled for quite a while, produced the book. The clerk handed it to the Justice who examined it. "But there's nothing here", he said to her.

"Oh, there is, there is", she said. "I had savings in, you see, only they're all out at the moment. I can borrow treble that if I want to", she said, waving expansively, reassuring and smiling.

"I'm sorry", said the justice. "Refused."

She smiled no more. "My daughter will do it, then", she said fearfully. "Maybe your daughter doesn't want to go bail", said the justice. "Oh, she does, she does so", said the woman, looking round at her daughter, who shook her head, knowing she was technically worth nothing. The woman left the stand, shaken, unsure. The court rose.

The trio sat there, then went out the door. As they went into the courtyard, the policeman they had rebuked met them. "How did it go", he asked them. "No good? Do you not know any shop-keepers?" he asked them.

No, no. They all shook their heads. They wouldn't ask anybody. They didn't want anyone to know. They didn't want to ask a shopkeeper, who had money and didn't know their son too well, to offer himself as guarantor for the son they knew all their lives, but couldn't guarantee because they had no cash — or liquid assets — or viable securities — such as stocks and shares, or gilt-edged bonds.

Both she and her husband worked, the women told me. They had worked all their lives. She had withdrawn the savings for her daughter's wedding. Why weren't they accepted? They had heard noises in the house at four the previous morning, and thought it was some of his friends come to see the son. They heard doors slamming shut. When the son, who was unemployed, had not returned home by noon that day, they had gone to the police station. He had been sent to jail for four months that morning, they were told, on an assault charge. He was appealing, and the bail was £80. Where would he be now, they wondered? "In the Bridewell", I said, "or maybe Mountjoy". And where was Mountjoy? It was too late, I told them. Four o'clock. They'd have to try tomorrow. Did they have no relatives who owned a car or a house? No, they said, no-one. They wondered what they could do. "Will he have to stay in jail?", the mother asked. "Yes," said the girl, bitterly. They looked frightened.

1 March 1973

Horse trading

She was worth the bail money, she said. She owned two horses.

"Horses? What sort of horses?" The Justice's voice

rose to a whinny.

"Horses," said the woman, looking nervously at him.

"But what sort of horses?" asked Justice Ó hUadhaigh peevishly.

"Working horses," said the woman. She owned two, she said, and her sons owned others.

"Do your sons own the horses?" persisted the Justice, who is a man.

"I own two of the horses," she said.

"Never mind how many you own," snapped the Justice. He thought for a second. "What colour are they?" he pounced on her.

The woman looked him straight in the face. She gave the colours of the horses, betraying no emotion. The Justice repeated the colours, and then asked her which colour was the pony. The woman steadily described the colour of the pony. They were used for drawing coal. The Justice wondered if a young pony could draw coal.

"Horse-owner," he murmured to himself. "All right. Accept in £90."

18 June 1975

Head of household

A father came forward to bail out his son, in the sum of £100. He was unemployed and received £20 a week social security benefit for himself and his six children and his wife. No, he had none of the assets required by Justice Ua Dhonnchadha. "But," he said levelly. "I have offered my head to the faculty of anthropology of the Royal College of Surgeons, who will pay £350 for it, and my body, after my death. In that way I have provided for the future. That is my asset." The man who offered his very head as posthumous security towards the freedom of his son was refused.

18 July 1974

Credit in the dock

The youth had been in custody for a week, and he wished to get back to his job where he had spent four years learning his trade. He told District Justice Ó hUadhaigh, in Dublin District Court 4, that he wanted to appeal the 12-month sentence imposed on him for taking away, and crashing, someone else's car.

His father came forward as bails person. Was he worth £110? the justice asked him. "I'm a docker. Yes, I'm worth it", said the father, confident as any docker.

"But have you liquid assets? Money in the bank or Post Office or anything like that?", asked the justice. "I had a lotta money in the bank but I was sick for a while and I'll be resuming work soon", said the father, "I'm good for £500 any time", he finished confidently.

"You mean in an overdraft if you wanted it?", asked the justice. "Ah, yes, the bank would give it to me", said the father proudly.

"But have you any money in the bank at the moment?", asked the justice. "Through me being out sick I had to withdraw the money," the father faltered. "But I have a good job, you know", he picked up.

"Well, that's good too", the justice said. "Were you made redundant?". "I'm waiting to be. I'm over 65 you know", said the father.

"Oh, are you?", asked the justice. The man did not look it. "Well, but, at the moment you're not worth £110." "It's only a matter of months till the union fix up the redundancy and I'll be worth a lot more than a hundred", said the father, confident as any life-long docker with the union behind him.

"But you're not worth it now. I'll have to refuse you", said the justice to the working man.

4 July 1975.

12

Chapter 2
Resisting the Guards

The two men were accused of obstruction of the gardai, assault and resisting arrest. Smith told Justice Ó hUadhaigh in Dublin District Court 4 that he had seen one of the prosecuting gardai baton one of two arrested youths and drag him across O'Connell Street to a phone box outside a hotel. The man using the baton was in civilian clothes, and Smith had approached him to ask if he was in fact a garda. "He told me to eff off, that it was none of my business. He continued to drag the youth along the ground, and stopped at the hotel. My companion Brown asked the garda for his number again, and the garda grabbed him by the lapels. Jones then called the garda a pig when he saw him grab Brown, and Jones lost his head and spat at the garda. The garda let go Brown's lapel, hit Jones and knocked him to the ground. The squad car came then and the two arrested youths were put into the car. They then picked Jones up and put him into the car, too."

"There is a suggestion that you incited a crowd?" the defending solicitor asked.

"No," said Smith, "I didn't. I asked the garda what station he was taking Jones to, as Jones's girl-friend was frantic . . the three of us, me, the girl and Brown went to Store Street station. I went in there first and the garda when he saw me said: 'Lock him up.' I said 'What for?' and he said 'Lock him effin up.' I didn't resist. I was later charged."

"You had done nothing else all evening, to incite anyone?" the solicitor asked. "No, I would have been satisfied with the garda's co-operation," replied Smith.

The garda then asked Smith: "Did I at any stage let go of the prisoner? No? And I was able to hit Jones and knock him on the ground? Didn't you catch this other garda by the shoulder and incite the crowd? No? No further questions."

Justice Ó hUadhaigh then said to Smith: "Why'd you ask the garda for his number when you were told to fuck off and mind your own business? Any comment on that, why you asked for his number when you were told to mind your own business . . . All I'm asking is, when you asked if he was a garda, and were answered with abusive language and told to mind your own business, why a few seconds later did you ask for his number?"

"Because the other garda admitted they were gardai," replied Smith.

Jones the window cleaner then gave evidence. "That night we went into town for a meal, myself, Smith, Brown and my girl-friend. There was a bit of commotion in Abbey Street. This young bloke was being rowdy. I understand that the garda had to take him in, but I didn't agree with the way they were doing it.

"My friend, Brown, went to check if the men were gardai, because they were in plain clothes. I saw one of the guards with his hands on my friend's lapel, and I lost the head and called him a Special Branch bastard, and he thumped me to the ground, dragged me to the car and later put me in a cell. Then Smith came into the cell too, but I was in no fit condition to see what was going on . . . at first I thought it was just a street fight, but when I saw him take out the truncheon I knew he was a garda, and I just didn't agree with the way he was doing it."

The garda cross-questioned him: "You said I struck you on the chin, but you didn't give that in evidence. Why'd you say you were thrown to the ground?"

"I didn't say that. The Justice said it," said Jones.

The Justice got very angry, and said Jones had clearly said "thrown," but Jones said no; he had said "thumped."

"Maybe my hearing is defective," said the Justice. "I definitely said thumped," reiterated Jones, "and I've got the scar on my inside lip to prove it".

"Why'd you say 'Special Branch bastard?' Did you not realise the effect that would have on the crowd," asked the garda.

"It would have less effect than the sight of a youth being batoned," intervened the solicitor.

"Why'd you spit on me?" asked the garda.

"I'd never done anything like that before. I'd like to apologise for that," said Jones. "That's fair enough," said Justice Ó hUadhaigh.

Brown then gave evidence. "Well, I was coming along with the two accused. Two youths were taken away by two men in white coats. One of the lads tried to break away, and the policeman kept hold of him. He tried to break away again, and the guard took out his baton and beat him, and he fell to the ground, and the guard kicked him and dragged him along the ground to the phone box. I asked the guard for his number, and he said 'no,' and the other guard came out of the phone-box, and I said 'You've no right to treat the young lad like that,' and he grabbed me by the lapel and said it was none of my business; he squeezed my throat and nearly throttled me, then he let me go, and I saw Jones on the ground, and then he was put in the squad car. We went to the police station, and the guard saw Smith and said: 'Lock him up,' and I protested. The guard told me to file a complaint if I objected, and I asked where I could do it, and he said if I didn't get out he'd lock me up, too."

"And you did nothing about it since?" asked Justice Ó hUadhaigh.

"I was afraid to return," said Brown.

The girl then took the stand: "There were two youths at a paint-shop kicking the window. Two plain-dressed men grabbed them, took them away, and one tried to escape. The second time he tried the garda took something from his pocket and just battered him to the ground, and dragged him across the street. I didn't know if the youth was unconscious or not; he was covered in blood, and the garda had blood on his coat, too. The squad car came and Jones was knocked to the ground, and taken to the station. We went after them, and when the guard saw Smith he took him, too, and when Brown asked what for? the guard said: 'If you don't get out you'll be behind bars, too.'"

No questions, said the prosecuting garda.

"Jones had pleaded guilty to assault, I'll mark the other charges withdrawn," said Justice Ó hUadhaigh. "I'll dismiss the assault against Smith, convict him of obstruction, dismiss the resist."

Smith had no previous convictions, said the garda, and Jones was fined £2 years ago for interfering with the mechanism of a car.

"The guard had prosecuted his case without the assistance of the State Solicitor's office," said Justice Ó hUadhaigh. "He's a youngish guard, and so is the guard who accompanied him, and they were opposed by a very experienced solicitor. Gardai have to operate under very difficult conditions . . . the garda drew his baton when his prisoner tried to escape a second time. Batons are not ornaments; they are issued for a purpose, for use when necessary. In fact, this guard did use his baton, I accept that he did, and had to drag the youth across the street. There were a large number of people, about ten, no doubt fairly interested which of course they're entitled to be but Smith and Jones went further. Jones spat at the guard, and was man enough to admit it here . . . the only duty of a member of the public, if a person is trying to escape, and he's not satisfied with the way the guard performed his duties, is to go to the station and make a complaint, not to the guard, but to a superior officer. If he's genuine he should stay there and ask to see the superintendent — if he's genuine. The third witness says he was throttled: he did nothing about it. He went to the station and says that he was told if he made a complaint he'd be locked up. I don't think that happened; I don't accept it at all; I think this thing was made up by people intent on trouble. On the independent evidence of the lady, a lad was trying to put his boot through a window . . . there's a lot of nonsense talked, and no evidence that the guard did other than he was entitled to do. The lady says there was blood on the prisoner, the first mention of it in this case. One would think it was the Battle of Waterloo or something; one would imagine that the very experienced solicitor would have taken this up.

"There's an anti-police element growing up in this city, and this is typical evidence of it here today. If a garda exceeds his duty, well, everyone exceeds his duty — I'm not saying this guard exceeded his duty — but no one is infallible, everybody makes mistakes. If there had been a genuine grievance — but there was no genuine grievance — these two were there to make trouble. Six months' imprisonment for each."

2 May 1973

Trying to be nice

He had gone to the home with the purpose of interviewing the accused's son, the guard told District Justice Good in Dublin District Court 6. He could have produced a warrant, or arrested the youth on the spot, but he was trying to be nice about it. The man, who did not think there was anything nice about the guard coming to take away his son, had demanded production of a warrant. This was his right, he thought. The matter came to court to be resolved.

The man was accused of wilfully obstructing the guard. "I knocked at the door and a child came out and I asked if his mother or father were in," said the guard. "I went into the hallway and the father came out and I said I wanted to interview his son in connection with inquiries we were making. He asked if I had a warrant. I said I hadn't, and he said he would take his son down to the station at seven that evening.

"I refused this and pointed out that I could arrest the son on the spot. I could see the youth I wanted standing in the kitchen. The father said he couldn't let me in without a warrant. Rather than start an argument I went out to the balcony and called to my colleagues to bring up the warrant. We in fact had a warrant to search the house, but we didn't want to do that. While I was on the balcony the father closed the door, and the youth I wanted escaped out the window."

"Did he get away?" asked the justice.

"No, he was arrested by other guards who were stationed out the back. Later that evening, when the father called down to the station, I arrested him.

"When I read out the charge he replied, 'I told you I would bring him down after tea.'"

"Do you want to ask the guard any questions?" asked the justice.

"No," said the man, "he's telling the truth."

The Justice invited him to tell his own story. He took the witness stand.

"I have a large family of 12," he said, "and eight of them are school-going. We were getting the kids ready that morning when the detective banged on the door, and said he wanted to interview my son, Paddy. I said we were getting the kids ready for school and I'd bring him round to the station later. Then I asked him if he had a warrant.

"I thought you needed one to get into a house. All my kids were milling around and there was general disturbance. The detective suddenly said 'All right', and he went out of the flat and I closed the door, and the next thing my son went out the window."

"But you knew the detective wanted to arrest your son?" asked the Justice.

"Interview him, not arrest him," corrected the man. "He didn't want to arrest him."

"But the moment you closed the door," said the Justice, "your son got away. You are making your own story sound very simple. The guards were only doing their duty after all."

"I know that, yes," said the man.

"Why didn't you co-operate?" asked the Justice.

"Well, I know now I was wrong," said the man.

"Oh, you realise that?" said the Justice. "You know now that you were very foolish? You wouldn't be here now if you had done what the guard wanted you to do.

You gave them an awful lot of trouble, didn't you?"

The very foolish man who had not done what the guards wanted him to, and who had caused them an awful lot of trouble early in the morning, said, "If I'd thought I was guilty of anything I would hardly have gone down to the station later. I never thought I'd be arrested."

The Justice convicted.

He had never been in trouble before, the guard said, and he added, "I'm not concerned with the penalty, Justice, I'd just prefer he knew the position."

"It must be brought home to anybody who interferes with the Gardai that they cannot get away with it," lectured the Justice. "You just cannot do it. You realise that now, don't you?"

"I do now," said the man.

"I'll find the facts proved and apply the Probation of Offenders Act," said the Justice.

17 July 1974

Charges against injured man

"So the only way you felt you could show contempt for the two guards was to spit in their faces after, you say, they had struck you several times," said District Justice Good to the man in the witness box of Dublin District Court.

"Yes," said the man, "and that seemed to infuriate them even more. I was badly beaten after that and knocked to the ground."

"But you spat on them?" asked the justice.

"After they had struck me," said the man.

"One guard struck you?" asked the justice.

"Several struck me," said the man. "They told me to shut up and I said no, so one struck me, and I spat at him, and then one of his colleagues hit me and I spat at him too. As a result of my injuries, justice, I was off work for a week, with headaches and that. I'm suggesting to you that it was not possible for me to have sustained those injuries by being dragged on the floor as

AN LEABHARLANN
INSTITIÚID TEICNEOLAÍOCHTA
LEITIR CEANAINN
340

500 38327

19

they said."

"I remember you saying you had to go to hospital," said the justice. "But weren't you being violent?" asked the justice. "According to the guards you had to be dragged into the station."

"Under no circumstances was I dragged anywhere," said the man firmly.

"The explanation of the guard is that you had to be dragged in, and you fell to the floor," said the justice. He invited the guard to cross-examine.

"This man says he didn't struggle, justice," said the guard, "but he did."

"Guard, if I may respectfully suggest, you should cross-examine the witness, not make a statement," said the justice. "He's told his story. It's up to you to examine him on that story."

"I put it to you that you struggled," said the guard to the man.

"I did not," said the man.

"I put it to you that you attempted three times to escape from the patrol car," said the guard.

"Is that true?" the justice asked the man.

"No," said the man, "it's not true. There was some kind of a thing on the door. Maybe it was nervous reaction or something, but I was touching it like, you know, and the guard told me to stop . . . I was only fiddling with it. I wasn't trying to escape. You could hardly jump out of a car going at so many miles an hour, justice."

"It does happen," said the justice. "People have jumped out of cars before, you know."

"I don't know, your honour," said the man.

They discussed the object he had been fiddling with. The man had not the vocabulary to describe it. It was not the handle of the door, he said, it was a thing at the top of the door. The justice said he had a vague idea what he meant.

The man's brother was called.

"My brother went into the bar," he said, "and I followed him and I heard the manager tell him to get out or he'd be thrown out. My brother said that he would walk out. The manager picked up a baton or truncheon then, and swiped at him, and he ducked, and the manager swiped again and caught him on the shoulder, or the side of the arm. My brother ran out, and on his way picked up an ashtray.

"He threw it over his head, and it smashed the mirror. I followed him out. The barman then came after me with a hurley and thumped me. My brother was walking up the road bleedin' — no, Justice, I don't know how that happened — and I stayed outside the pub arguing with the barman, saying that I hadn't done anything. We talked for about 15 minutes. Then I went to my brother and as we walked up the road the police came in a car and said: 'Come over here a minute,' and the manager was there, and he identified us, and the police took us to the station. There was not a struggle of any kind in the car.

"My brother was playing with this thing that goes up and down — you know the things on cars that go up and down, and the guard kept saying 'leave that alone!' . . . we got into the station and the minute we got out of the car two guards pulled batons. My brother asked for his solicitor and was told to shut up. He kept asking and there were about ten guards there, and he was punched in the face. Two guards held him, two kicked him, and another gave him digs. There were some other people in the station and I went over to them to ask their names as witnesses to what was happening and the guards were dragging me across the floor by the hair and kicking me in the ribs . . . one guard took off his helmet and hit my brother. He was spitting blood as well. Not spitting blood at them, the blood was spitting out of his mouth, but he did spit at them . . . after an hour they let us out and we went to hospital."

"Yes," said the justice. "I remember that in court the next day your brother asked me to take note of his injuries, because, he said, they would have disappeared by the time the case was finally heard."

The defence solicitor made the point that charges against this brother of assault against the guards had later been withdrawn. The prosecuting guard said that both brothers had been named in the charge sheet, but that he had asked that the sheet be amended next day, and the second brother's name taken off.

The solicitor pointed out that this meant the second brother had been formally charged in the station that night, whatever about amendments in court the next morning, and that charges against the second brother of assaulting the guards had, therefore, been withdrawn.

The solicitor said that he "would not take up the time of the court by making a long address," and he pointedly sat down.

The justice dismissed charges against the first brother of assaulting the publican, but convicted him of breaking the mirror on his own admission. "The other charges concerning assault on the guards give one concern," he continued. "I assume the nature of the assault charge against him is that he spat in the guards' faces and that the coat and collar of one of the guards was grabbed by him. Quite frankly, I'm not completely happy about this case.

"No doubt the defendant was in a bad mood after the unfortunate events prior to his arrest." The justice then digressed for about 500 words on how the defendant should have known, and indeed did know, that a publican could refuse admission to a pub to whomsoever he wished, and that the defendant should have left the pub straight-away without argument.

"The guards then arrived and a rather ugly scene followed," said the justice, the account of which differed vastly between the guards and the defendant and his brother. "Rightly or wrongly, the defendant was by the time in a bad mood . . . whether or not he was denied access to a solicitor in the station was not put to the guards by the defence . . . the extraordinary feature of this case is that the next day in court the defendant invited me to take note of his injuries. I saw a cut over his left eye, necessitating four, no, six stitches, and both of his eyes were badly bruised. His lip was badly cut. Nobody can say he didn't suffer these injuries. The guards say they used no more force than was necessary. I don't know. The guards deny using batons. Frankly, I'm not at all happy about this case. As to assault on the guards, there is a genuine doubt and I'm dismissing the charges against this man."

He went on to fine the man, who was a labourer with two children and a pregnant wife, £10 for breaking the mirror, with payment of £45 damages. He gave him two months to pay or three months' imprisonment in default.

In deciding judgment after convicting the man of breaking the publican's mirror, it emerged that the man had spent two years in a children's reformatory in Connemara for housebreaking, and another 18 months there for a similar offence. He had also served six months for assaulting a guard in 1966, and 18 months for assaulting a guard and resisting arrest. He had been given six months in England for possession of an offensive weapon in 1965 and was twice deported from England after that. His last offence was in 1972.

The justice said that even had he known the man's record this would not have influenced him in his decision to dismiss the present charge of assaulting the guards, although the man had admitted to spitting in the guards' faces.

Nor was he convicted of assaulting the publican, who had assaulted him.

And that's where matters closed. The justice is not alone in his unhappiness about the "ugly events" of that night. How did the man get his injuries and what will be done about it?

25 March 1975

Just checking

A garda told District Justice Good in Court 6 that when he had stopped him, the defendant had replied that he had a grievance, and was being harassed by the police. He had then started shouting "intimidation", and the garda had tried to talk sense to him, and told him to go home. He would not do so, so the garda arrested him.

"What made you stop him?" the Justice asked. "I knew him" replied the garda, "he had previous convictions." "Did you have any reason to stop him?" queried the Justice. "No, no reason", said the garda, "I was just checking."

The defendant then gave his version. "For the last twelve months, everywhere I go, I am followed by these policemen. I'm just fed up being stopped and searched. When this guard searched me, I said that if he was going to search me I should be arrested and charged. So he arrested me."

"He tried to gather a crowd around", the garda came back. "He tried to incite them. But when I informed him that I was arresting him, he got very quiet, and he apologised to me in the station."

"If you'd been more co-operative you wouldn't be here now, isn't that right?", the Justice asked the defendant.

"There's a garda here now in this court who stopped me last week," said the defendant, "and two Special Branch men. Everywhere I go I'm stopped and searched."

"I don't think there's much in this case, garda", said the Justice. "I don't think there's too much. The defendant may have raised his voice, but, however, he can go away."

3 March 1973

Fucking and blinding

He had been walking along the street with his colleague, the guard told District Justice O hUadhaigh, in Dublin District Court 4, when his attention was brought to the group on the opposite side of the street by "a lot of language. Fuck this and fuck that, and an awful lot of language similar to that, justice. It was midnight in a residential area. There were a number of people at windows looking out."

In the dock sat four youths who did not look demure. On the other hand, they did not look like desperados.

"So the other guard and I approached them and spoke to them about their conduct. I asked Smith for his name after I had brought the matter to their attention. He refused, saying 'What do you want my bleedin' name for?' I told them they would have to quit their carry-on, justice, and they didn't, so I arrested them and brought them to the station . . ." Smith was invited to cross-question. He looked the most demure of the youths, in that he wore a regular jacket and tie and had a carefully tended moustache, if one judges by such things.

"He asked me for my name, and he wouldn't say what for, justice. Then I gave him my name," said Smith.

The justice translated this into a question to the guard.

"He didn't give his name at the scene," replied the guard. "The others were willing to give his name for him, but I had asked him specifically," he finished officiously.

"I gave him my name as they put me into the car. Or I gave it to the other fella, I don't remember which," said Smith. "There were two of them there." "We know there were two of them. The guard referred to his colleague," said the justice. He invited the others to cross-question. "He told us to stop the language and we stopped the language," said Murphy.

"If they had moved on when we first approached them," the guard replied, "we would have let them off with a caution. But they said they couldn't understand why we had approached them about their conduct."

"No," said Murphy, "we said we were going home, and he said we were getting into the squad car, and we said fair enough, and we didn't resist arrest."

"You're not charged with resisting arrest," said the justice, shortly. "We were just after leaving the club," was White's contribution to the cross-examination.

"That's evidence. I invited questions," said the justice.

"Did I use abusive language to you?" White asked the guard in a simple inspiration.

"It was used collectively," the guard hedged.

"He says did he use it to you? Did he address abusive language to you?" the justice pinned him.

"No. Not to me," the guard admitted.

The second guard testified: "They were shouting and roaring and fucking and blinding. The language was very, very choice," he said in a young affronted voice

. . . "Smith seemed to think we shouldn't ask his name, that he knew his rights, and that he was not going to give it," he continued.

The other lads volunteered Smith's name, but Smith himself "was not going to give his name, not to me, not to the other guard", his voice rose, "but he gave it himself, later, in the station," he finished in satisfaction, his authority re-established.

"He's not charged with refusing to give his name," the justice defused the situation. "That's only an indication of the frame of mind," he bolstered the guard's falling face, "though it was hardly likely to cause a breach of the peace," he concluded drily. It was nearly four in the rainy afternoon, and there were many more cases to be heard.

"Yes, but he seemed to think —" the guard accused again. "Never mind what he was thinking. He might have been thinking you were the archangel," the justice said abruptly.

"I gave my name," said Smith plaintively.

"Ah, don't mind that," said the justice, irritation showing. The other three youths had no questions to ask.

"Convict all," said the justice swiftly. "Now, what is known about them, guard?" Murphy had 11 previous convictions, said the guard.

"Murphy is the big one?" The justice indicated the biggest youth. "Yes. They include most things, housebreaking, larceny, unauthorised taking of motor-cars, offences under the Road Traffic Act," the guard chattily profiled the classic anti-social record.

Murphy was an unmarried bricklayer.

"White had seven previous convictions," said the guard. "Oh, had he?" the justice sat up. He looked at White, whose curiously-shaped head was such as to attract vulgar attention. "Did you have an accident one time to your head?" The justice drew attention to the youth's appearance. White nodded his poor head.

"Black has no previous convictions, and Smith has four," the guard finished.

"Right" said the justice. "Black, fined two pounds. White, Smith and Murphy, fined two pounds each, 14 days to pay, and bound to the peace for 12 months in bonds of £5 each, and one independent surety each of £150, the bonds to be entered into within 14 days, or in default six months' imprisonment each."

"Thank you, justice", said one youth.

The justice looked at them.

"If you don't enter into the bonds, you will be picked up, arrested, and locked away in Mountjoy Prison for six months," he said.

It's actually quite difficult if you come from the working class to find independent bails-people worth £150.

2 December 1975

Disobedience

He had seen the two defendants outside a chip-shop at midnight, and had asked them to go away, the garda said. They had stood there, and he asked them again. They moved back into the chip-shop. Five minutes later he saw them across the road and he asked them to move on. Smith "came up towards me, threw one chip towards me, he had been eating it, then he threw the bag of chips on the ground in front of me, I walked away, and five minutes later I asked them again and they refused to go. I was called away, but when I came back 20 minutes later, they were outside the chip-shop, and I asked them to go, but they refused. Smith used bad language. He told me to eff off. He told me I was an effing bastard. He started calling the cops names. Jones didn't say anything, except that he wouldn't go away", the garda complained, "but Smith is always causing trouble."

Had Smith anything to say? Justice Good asked. "It's all a load of lies," said the defendant, briefly. "What the garda says is a load of lies?" asked the Justice.

"Yes", said Smith. "I was talking to this guy all night" (he indicated his co-defendant). "We were talking football. I only get up on weekends, once every two months, I don't get a chance to enjoy myself. I was talking to him at the chippie when a squad-car stopped and took me and him in."

"Is there any truth in what he says?", the Justice asked the garda. "He's leaving out the details", said the garda. "Four times I asked him to move, and four times he refused." "You only asked me twice", said the defendant, "and I moved the second time."

"Why didn't you move the first time?", the Justice asked the youth who had refused to move, immediately he was told to, by a garda. "Because I was eatin' chips and talking," the defendant said, not unreasonably.

"He threw chips at me", said the garda.

"I threw me chips away 'cos I was gettin' sick", said the defendant.

"He wasn't getting sick", said the garda. "He was pretending to be sick and trying to create a scene. There were twelve fellows watching and laughing after me."

"Look," said the defendant to the Justice, "I've nothing more to say. It's just the truth. I'm down in the Curragh, I only get up every few weeks, and I can't enjoy myself. I went to the chipper and I was told to move on and I got a box on the ears."

"Who gave you the box?" asked the Justice. "The guard did", said the boy.

"Now are you sure you weren't being too difficult?" asked the Justice. "Are you sure? The gardai would be only too happy to see you move on".

"He was in jail two years ago", the garda said.

"I think you were being a bit difficult", the Justice said. (He was speaking to the defendant). "If you had done what the garda told you, you wouldn't be here today. Are you working?"

"I'm a private in the Army", the youth said.

"You're right, garda, in saying that if Smith had moved on, Jones would have gone on too. Jones, I'm satisfied that you behaved yourself, and didn't give cheek to the guards. You conducted yourself as you should have. I'm satisfied that if Smith had gone on, you would have too. Charges dismissed. Smith, I fine you £1, fourteen days to pay, or fourteen days in default".

If Smith had stayed silently where he was, would he have been all right?

Why was Jones brought to court, thereby losing a day's pay? Why did the garda tell Smith to move on? Must we do exactly what gardai tell us? Why?

3 March 1973

Chapter 3
Sex & Drugs

He had seen the defendant in the laneway with three juveniles, the guard told District Justice Good in Dublin District Court No. 4. He had no idea what they were doing at this time, and so did not stop the man when he first came out of the laneway and passed on up the square. The guard questioned the juveniles, who explained to him that the man had paid them some money and interfered with them.

The guard stopped the man when he returned to his car, and the man admitted that the information was correct and had made a statement later in the station. "You say he interfered with them?" questioned the Justice. "He had paid them to masturbate him," explained the guard. He then read out the man's statement.

The guard said that the three youths, aged 10 to 14, were itinerants, and he had been unable to contact their parents, who were very hard to locate. He had seen the youths every night around the town "begging and so forth".

The man was in his late forties, the guard said, and had his own business, which was quite good. He was single and had no previous convictions. The explanation he gave was that he had had some drink taken and had on the spur of the moment forgotten himself.

"How do you account for this filthy behaviour?" the Justice asked the defendant.

"It wasn't premeditated," he replied. "It had hardly happened when I realised what had happened to myself."

"But you must have known," said the justice.

"They were standing around me you see. Two of them had their hands in my pockets," said the man.

"That's no excuse for allowing children to do what they did to you," said the justice.

"I didn't ask them," said the man.

"Do you know anything about his activities?" the justice asked the guard.

"He told me he's going steady at the moment and hopes to get married," replied the guard.

"Hopes to get married? How old is he now?" asked the justice, and the guard told him.

"Well, I don't know what to do with you," the justice said to the defendant. "You have committed a very serious offence, apart from a filthy one. Even though these children are members of the itinerant class, you shouldn't have been a party to it. The only thing in your favour is that you have no previous convictions."

"He seems to be very straight-forward. He didn't deny it. He admitted it to me and was very co-operative," interjected the guard.

"Were you ever under medical care? Have you ever been treated for any complaint?" asked the justice. The man shook his head.

"Taking account of your previous good character, and good employment, and the fact that you have no previous convictions," remarked the justice, "I will — I could send you to prison — but I'm satisfied this was an isolated case. Are you satisfied of that, guard? I will fine you £5, with 14 days to pay, or two months' imprisonment in default. Furthermore, you will be bound over for 12 months, and it will be a condition of the bond that you do not interfere, or molest, or indecently assault children of tender years."

"I've never done it before," said the man.

"And you'll never do it again?" asked the justice.

"Never again," said the man.

"If you enter into the bond you'll hear no more about it," said the justice.

26 January 1974

Consenting males bound over

Dublin District Court 4 was cleared of the public. Two men entered the dock and sat apart, like strangers, before District Justice Ua Donnchadha. The wife of one of the men sat in a corner at the back of the court. Solicitors for both men said they would be pleading guilty.

As the result of a complaint, the prosecuting guard said, he had gone to the public toilets in a certain area. After waiting there a while, the door to one of the cubicles opened and one man came out. The guard saw a second man still inside the cubicle.

He stopped both accused and spoke to them outside the toilets. At that time they denied everything. Later they admitted all. The guard proposed to read their statements.

"In view of the wife's presence in court, perhaps we need not hear the statements," one solicitor delicately suggested.

"If the wife does not wish to hear she can go outside," the justice said. "This is a public court."

The wife remained and listened to the two accounts of the men's sexual activities together in the toilet.

Neither had any previous convictions.

A psychiatrist for the younger man, aged 25, was called to testify. The defendant had been referred to him by a priest.

"He has been attending me regularly, five days a week, since this happened," the doctor said. "The conclusion I came to is that first he is very sincere . . . I am very slow to come to conclusions about cases which are pending in court.

"But in this case I am convinced of his sincerity. He did not think in fact that he could be treated, and was wrongly advised to this effect by a psychiatric nurse. Depending on his desire, he can be treated . . . with psycho-therapy . . . no medication is being used".

Was it fair to suggest that he was sexually immature, the solicitor asked.

He was, the doctor agreed.

The justice interjected to wonder why men behaved in

this manner. "It's a completely unnatural performance," the justice said. "Normally at his age, young men are more interested in people of the opposite sex."

There was a total pattern, involving the young man's back-ground, which explained it, the doctor said. "But he did have a girl-friend and he dreams about girls. However, he lacks self-confidence and feels inferior . . ."

"Would you say that he could have a fruitful relationship with a member of the opposite sex? That he could marry and have children?" the solicitor asked helpfully.

"Yes, indeed," the doctor said.

The other solicitor went into the case history of the married man. He had married two years ago, and unfortunately his job entailed his being away from home very often. "The only conclusion I can come to," said the solicitor, "is that he was suffering from depression."

"He'd had a few drinks on that evening . . . a conviction would result in the loss of his good job . . . on the strength of the job he and his wife had bought a house with heavy mortgage commitments.

"His wife says they are happily married. She is a very nice person obviously. So is he . . . I think I can assure you, justice, that there will be no repetition of this incident "

The justice pointed out that the statements implied a prior association. "They'll have to break up such associations," the justice warned. "It's extraordinary how these types seem to gravitate to each other. In other countries, I understand, this is not an offence between adult consenting males."

"And no-one actually saw them do it," the solicitor came in.

"Well," said the justice finally. "It's against the law here. The law's the law and they broke the law. One answer is prison obviously. If they had been dealt with before a jury they could have gotten penal servitude, strange as it seems to say. In the interest of justice, I will bind them in their own bonds to keep the peace for a year.

"It goes without saying that their association must break up and there must be no repetition of this."

12 September 1975

Indecent Exposure

In Court 4 a pregnant woman was going bail for her husband who had been charged with indecent exposure. Her mother escorted her to the witness box. The woman, young, and red-faced, squeezed anxiously into her seat. She did not fully understand what was happening. She was also partly deaf.

Justice Ó hUadhaigh asked her if she was worth £50. She nodded her head and shook it and put her hand to her ear. She became agitated and distressed. The Justice repeated the question into the microphone. Had she her own house? No, she said half a house. She lived in a flat. Her mother encouraged her with smiles and pleas.

The Justice asked her not to worry. The woman's face squeezed into agony. It was hard to hear, harder to understand, she was pregnant, and her husband was locked up.

So she cried. Not large swelling tears. There was misery and ignorance and fear in her poor twisted red face; stuck pregnant in a witness box, her mother nodding below, the Justice adjudicating above.

We all watched, the Justice, the mother, the policemen, and I as she fretfully cried, and twisted in her trap. The Justice could not stand it. He hurriedly accepted her bond, and left the Bench, to go to lunch. The policemen left, I left too. The woman and her mother went timidly and in shame to the bail office.

11 January 1974

Never mind the assault

"I met the person concerned, Paddy, I don't know his second name, at the discotheque", the woman told District Justice Good in Dublin District Court 4. "I had been introduced to him before. We went back to his flat for a cup of coffee between half-past two and three in the morning. Then I left the flat, taking my handbag, and, as I was walking along the balcony, the hallway, he followed me."

"Did you get your coffee?", the Justice broke in.

"No, we didn't have coffee after all", said the woman.

"Oh, I see", said the Justice, tactfully.

"I was only in the flat for 10 minutes", she said.

"Was there any reason why you didn't get coffee?", asked the Justice delicately.

"There was", she said hesitantly. "He started . . . messing, like . . . and I didn't want . . ."

"You felt that it wasn't for coffee he had asked you back to the flat" said the Justice solemnly.

She nodded. "He followed me down the balcony and grabbed me by the back of the hair, pulled my hair back, and said that if I didn't go back to his flat with him that he would throw me over the balcony. My bag fell to the ground and he grabbed it and said that I would have to come back for that anyway".

"Were you holding the bag by the handle, or was it over your arm, or what?", asked the Justice.

"It's a shoulder-bag", she explained, "and the strap comes undone sometimes. He didn't break it, the strap just came loose and it fell to the ground. I was crying by that time, you know. I was a bit frightened, like. So I went on down and rang the police, and they came back to the flat with me and he handed the bag over".

"What was in your bag?", asked the Justice.

"There was a brown leather purse with 40 odd pence in it", she said, "and some papers, and a comb. Nothing really valuable."

"Was anything missing?", asked the Justice.

"No", she said.

"How long had you known this man?", asked the Justice.

"I met him three months ago, but I only saw him about three times since then", she said.

"Had you ever kept company with him?" asked the Justice.

"Never", she said firmly.

"And were you dancing with him at this discotheque?", asked the Justice.

"Yes, we had a couple of dances, I think", she said. "I spent most of the evening with him".

The Justice invited the man to cross-examine her.

"She told me she couldn't pay for a taxi", he began. The Justice asked him to confine himself to questions, for the moment.

"Isn't it true that you left your handbag in the flat when you went out?", the man asked her.

"That's not true", she said.

"Well, it is", he said. "I was making coffee".

"I went out, and I took my coat off the table and my bag, and you came after me and said 'Who do you think you are walking out on me like this' ", she said.

"I'm a bit stunned. I don't know what to ask her", said the man helplessly to the Justice.

"Take your time", the Justice comforted him. "I'll give you ample opportunity to think. Then you can tell me your own story".

"Was I making coffee?", the man asked her.

"I never saw you making coffee, no," she said.

The man sat down.

"Come into the witness box and take the oath and tell me the whole story. Tell me your version of it", the Justice invited him.

"I met her in the club, and we had a few drinks and dances", the man said. "She told me she'd met me before, but I couldn't remember it. I belong to a pop group, so she might have seen me with them. I asked her if there was anybody with her and she said no, so I sat down beside her. She talked depression all the time, as if she was depressed. She said she was fed up most of the time. I said we all get fed up at times, but sometimes we have to cheer up and enjoy ourselves, especially in a place of entertainment".

"What was the nature of your invitation to her?", asked the Justice.

"I asked her if she would like to come back to my flat for a cup of coffee", he said. He lived alone in the flat.

"So you brought her back for the purpose of having a cup of coffee", said the Justice thoughtfully.

"Well, after 10 minutes or so I put the kettle on for a cup of coffee", the man continued.

"How did you prepare the coffee? Was it instant coffee?", asked the Justice. "Ground coffee", said he. The Justice nodded appreciatively.

"Well, she was still going on about being depressed, so I said to her 'Have a cup of coffee and cheer up', and I was in the kitchenette and I heard the door bang."

"The door of the kitchenette or the flat door?", asked the Justice.

"The front door", said he, "and I came out and I saw her bag on the table, and I thought she must have gone out for a while. The reason why, I just don't know".

"Are you sure?", asked the Justice.

"I'm sure", he said emphatically. "Well, anyway, I'd tried talking to her, and she seemed depressed and so on, and I wasn't going to start running streets after her, or anything, so I left the bag on the table and went up to bed, and then the two police officers called looking for her bag, I lifted it off the table and gave it to them."

"Did you think she had gone home?", asked the Justice.

"Maybe. I didn't know where she lived. She'd told me during the night, but I'd forgotten. The thing is, if I was going to steal a person's handbag I wouldn't bring her back to my flat, would I? And I never assaulted anybody in my life."

"Never mind the assault. It wasn't serious", said the Justice. "But she says you took the bag and said she would have to come to the flat for it. Is she not telling the truth in that respect? I mean, did you want her to come back to the flat, in fact? Be frank now."

"Well, she had said that she'd no taxi money, and I thought she would have come back", said the man. "I hadn't much money myself, but I would have gone down the street to my sister's place to borrow it."

"Did you threaten to throw her over the balcony?", asked the Justice.

"No", said the man.

"Were you perfectly sober?", asked the Justice.

"I was, yes," he replied.

"She suggests that you invited her back to the flat for more than coffee", said the Justice.

"She came back willingly", said the man. "I didn't try anything out of the way with the girl."

"Well, in your favour, she didn't say that you did", said the Justice.

He called the woman back to the stand and asked her if she stood for her sworn oath that he had threatened to throw her over the balcony. She did.

"Are you satisfied that nothing was taken from your bag?", asked the Justice.

"Yes. I don't think his object was to steal the bag. I think he just wanted to get me back in the flat", she said.

"This is a most unusual case", said the Justice. "The defendant is charged with stealing, and I must make up my mind whether his purpose was to steal. I am satisfied there was no *mens rea* — which means intent in his mind — though he may have had other ideas in his mind which didn't work according to plan. As far as I am concerned I don't think he is guilty. Charge dismissed."

The man left the dock.

"What about the assault?" asked the guard.

"Oh, I don't think the assault was serious", said the Justice as the man stopped at the court door, "Dismiss, Probation of Offenders Act".

This being International Women's Year, I find the case interesting for a number of reasons. The woman said that she had been frightened on the balcony after the man had pulled her hair and threatened to throw her over it. The Justice found the assault "not serious". Does he think the woman was frightened because of the suggestions made to her in the flat? Suggestions are one thing. Hurtling over a balcony is something else. That's what frightened the woman, surely.

The case was not unusual. It is unusual only in that it came to court. Of course, you'll all be telling me he never intended to throw her over the balcony. And he certainly didn't intend to steal the bag. Quite so. But that he resorted to such tactics to get from her what she did not want to give leaves one wondering just what it is men are looking for, and what they think women might gain from it. The thing is, it happens all the time.   *15 January 1975*

Just one of those pimps

Her clothes, like her body, were without substance. Her face was as pale as her hair. The dock of Dublin District Court 4 was just another place to her. The guard told District Justice Good that he had arrested her at midday on foot of a warrant.

"Why didn't you turn up last time when you were remanded on bail?" the Justice asked her.

"I didn't get my lawyer," she said.

"Weren't you granted Free Legal Aid? Why didn't you go to see your lawyer?" asked the Justice.

"I didn't know where he lived," she said.

"Wasn't his address on the letter?" asked the Justice.

"Yes, but I didn't know where the place was," she said.

The guard said that the lawyer's letter had been sent to the address of the mother of the man she had been living with. She was now ready to go ahead with the case, without a lawyer. She intended to plead guilty.

There were two charges, the Justice pointed out. "That you, a common prostitute, were found loitering and importuning . . ." and that "you, a common prostitute, were found loitering for purposes of prostitution."

She pleaded guilty to the second charge, punishable by a fine. The first charge carried a sentence of imprisonment.

"I knew her to be a common prostitute," the guard described the pale young woman who sat in the dock. "On July 14th last year, I saw her approach a car and speak to the lone male occupant. She didn't go away with him. I approached her and arrested her. 'Nothing to say' was her answer to the charge."

"Do you want to say anything to me about this?" the Justice asked her. She shook her head.

"You merely shake your head?" the Justice asked. "Is this the life you are going to pursue? Are you going to carry on through life as a prostitute? What are you going to do?"

"I'm going to look for a job," she said briefly.

"How long have you been looking for a job?" asked

the Justice.

She stayed silent.

She had two previous convictions in 1975, the guard said.

"Strike out the first charge, which would have meant her going to jail," said the Justice. "Fined £2 on the second charge, 14 days to pay or seven days' imprisonment in default."

The young woman whom the men had described as a common prostitute left the dock.

She was replaced, later, by the man she had been living with. He pleaded guilty to living wholly or partly on the earnings of a prostitute. He was young, thin, and badly dressed. Two flying swallows adorned the backs of his hands. He asked to speak from the witness stand, on oath.

"I lived with her because she asked me to," he said. "She said she wouldn't live alone. I met her two years ago, when she was pretty down and out, living on the streets and so forth. She had a complaint. She suffered from TB. I told her I could get her into a convent for a while for a rest."

"A convent?" the startled Justice interrupted him.

"Yes," he continued. "She went into the convent and only stayed there three days. I asked her what she wanted to do then. She said she wanted to live in a flat. I took my money from the Labour Exchange and put her into a flat, but she wouldn't stay there either. Eventually she ended up in hospital for her TB. It's not that I wanted to stay with her. I wanted to be on my own but we lived together after that."

The guard had no questions to put in cross-examination. "He is pleading guilty," the guard explained.

However, he wished to read the man's statement which he proceeded to do.

"About two years ago I met her in O'Connell Street. We started going out together. At first she lived in a hostel. Then she lived in a flat with me as my common law wife. After six months a friend told me she was a prostitute. I hadn't been thinking how she spent her time. I asked her to stop going out on the town. She stopped for about four months. Then she started again. She told me to go and fuck myself if I didn't like it. We got into trouble with my family over it, and we had to start sleeping around, in old cars and things. We spent four nights of the week in bed and breakfasts. During this time she was a prostitute. She paid for the bed and breakfasts and the food we ate during the day. I was getting £7 off the Labour, and I gave £4 to my mother and father.

"She bought me cigarettes and shoes and clothes, and a watch and a ring, which I pawned. At the end of January, we fell out because I wanted her to stop going on the town. Then I met her in a certain area and I asked her to come back with me.

"I should say here that I was supposed to protect her from clients when she was doing business."

The guard finished the statement, and read out the man's previous convictions. One month's imprisonment from the Juvenile Court for a traffic offence. The Probation Act from the Juvenile Court for a traffic offence. Six months' imprisonment from the Juvenile Court for larceny in 1973. Six months' imprisonment from the Juvenile Court for larceny in 1970. Seven days' imprisonment from the Juvenile Court for larceny in 1972. The Probation Act for the unauthorised taking away of a car and a £1 fine for a similar offence, also from the Juvenile Court.

"I feel that deep down the defendant does care for this girl," the guard finished hesitantly.

"I do care, I want to look after her," the young man said.

"You're just one of those pimps. Six months' imprisonment," said the Justice shortly.

The young woman had already left the court.

31 March 1976

Hooked on cough mixture

They pleaded guilty to all the charges, the two youths told District Justice Good in Dublin District Court 4. They broke and entered a lock-up premises, damaged two windows and removed two prescriptions, the property of a doctor, together with bottles of vitamin tablets. One youth was 18; the other 17.

The 17-year-old had been on drugs since he was 14, the drug officer said.

"Drugs since he was 14," the justice shook his head.

"Cough mixture," the officer nodded.

"Cough mixture," the justice choked.

"If you take too much of it, you get a kick out of it," said the officer.

"I must confess I didn't know that," the justice composed himself. "What kind of kick?" he asked professionally.

"It stimulates you," said the officer.

"Does it stimulate you to the extent of —?" the justice hinted with an air of knowledge.

"Apparently so," said the officer.

"What exactly is the reaction?" the justice asked firmly.

"Well, you get elated," said the officer.

"Yeah, elated. Happy," the 17-year-old smiled happily, waving his hands in the air. "You get the cough mixture from any chemist's shop."

The second youth was on LSD, the officer said.

"Oh-ho," said the justice. "LSD. That's a hard drug," he stated firmly.

"Apparently on the night in question, 'Kelly' here, the youngest, stole his mother's valium tablets," said the officer.

"His mother's valium tablets," said the justice gravely.

"They took 19 tablets each and subsequently they broke into the doctor's place," said the officer.

"The idea being to procure more drugs on false prescriptions," the justice followed the trail.

"Well, justice," said the officer gently, "they admit themselves that on 19 tablets each, they didn't know what they intended to do."

Kelly had four previous convictions. Two years' probation from the juvenile court in 1972 for malicious damage. Probation in 1973 from the juvenile court for house-breaking and larceny. A period in Dundrum hospital for an offence I didn't catch. And a six-month prison sentence for malicious damage in 1975.

"White" had received the Probation Act for a minor offence from the juvenile court in 1971, and the Probation Act from the same court in 1972 for house-breaking. In 1972 he was fined £1 for obstructing a guard in the execution of his duty, and he had served six months' imprisonment in 1973 for house-breaking and larceny.

Kelly elected to tell his story under oath.

"I'd like to say, justice, that every time I get into trouble, I go on to drugs for a few days. About three years ago I met these two fellows in the housing estate where I live and they were on drugs, cough mixture and hash. They gave me cough mixture."

"May I say something?" the boy's mother called from the back of the court.

"Let the boy speak first," said the justice.

"Well, this cough mixture makes you feel good, justice. Really good, you know. You don't seem to need anything else really after you've had it. It's enough, justice. It makes you feel happy. I was happy, justice . . . it gives you a sense of, of, well-being . . . . I left the technical school after two years and I got a job as a van helper. I stayed at it for two or three months. I'd be in the lorry, you know, and I'd stop off somewhere and get the cough mixture. Then I couldn't stick the job any longer. Then I got another job as a van helper with a wine and spirit merchant."

"That wasn't the best job considering your condition," commented the justice.

"Ah, no, justice, it turns you off drink, that job," the boy reassured him.

"Then I got a job working with me father," the boy continued, "but he got fed up with me. He had an idea what was going on, you know."

"The cough mixture?" asked the justice. "And did he try to stop you?"

"Well, justice, the way it was," said Kelly. "I wasn't really listening to anything anyone had to say in those days. It's only in the last few months I've realised I had to stop this carry-on."

He felt he needed treatment, he said, and he would like to go to a live-in drug centre.

"My story is the same, justice," said White.

"No, everyone has their own story to tell, I'm always ready to listen to a man's story," said the justice.

"Well," White entered the witness stand, "I got onto this stuff, the cough mixture, though I haven't been on it as long as him. I got into bad company, justice. It started off when I went to London. There were these fellows, you know, and they said to me I might as well try it, so I said to myself I might as well try it, and I tried it. I felt the same as him. It made me happy, justice. Really happy, you know? I had a job here as a chef in a big hotel . . . yes, I know that was a good job, justice, but I was very young, and I had to start at three in the afternoon and finish at half past 10 at night, and I was missing out on life. I was young, justice, you know."

He got on to LSD and resumed the cough mixture in Dublin, but the chemists in the area began to catch on and started refusing to give it to them. It could be bought without prescription.

"I wish steps could be taken to prevent cough mixture getting into the hands of young men without a doctor's prescription," said the justice.

Kelly's mother took the witness stand. She looked strained and anxious, and fiercely caring for her son who sat in the dock below her.

"What I want to say about this cough mixture, justice," she said, "is that it is deadly. It's soul-destroying."

"I'm adopting that opinion too," said the justice gravely.

"If you take it for long enough," continued the mother, "you end up, to me, you end up, justice, as nothing. You're just a vegetable."

The justice assured her that the drug centre was an excellent place and he had heard excellent reports about it. He talked about tragic cases of drug addicts who had appeared before him in court, refused treatment, "and now they've gone beyond. They've passed away."

White's father took the stand.

"The truth as far as I understand," said the father, a small bright-eyed man, "and I am not a professional, justice, is that he never took those big drugs he talks about that he took in London.

"It's like a young lad that starts to drink. You can take four pints, so you tell everybody you can take six. I really believed he wasn't on those hard drugs. A drug addict? Justice, since he came back from London he's been a television addict. He never went out at night. A television addict, justice. We encouraged him to go out. He wouldn't go. Except this one night he went out and this happens."

The justice pointed out that the drug centre was a voluntary one. He had not the power to commit people there. He believed these "two decent frank lads" really wanted treatment, but it was a hard course, a difficult course, and they might not stick with it. They might just walk out. So he deferred judgment on the case for six months. If at the end of that time he got a report from the drug centre that the two youths had completed treatment successfully there he would adopt a lenient attitude.

If he got a report that they had not stayed there . . . well then. The two youths nodded.

And off they went to try to find a new way of happiness.
19 July 1975

Addiction no excuse

The defendant had already appeared in court the week before, and received a six-month sentence for the unauthorised possession of 27 sleeping-pills. Now he was charged with attempting to break and enter, and the assault of a woman. The incident had taken place last year. He lolled on the bench, his head thrown back on the partition behind him. At times he drifted into sleep, to come awake with a jerk. He had trouble focussing his red-rimmed eyes. I watched him all through the case and he was seldom capable of paying attention to the proceedings around him. His solicitor and father were there.

The woman testified that her bedroom door had opened

"and a figure came across the room, as if — I would say
he skipped across the room. I said 'Who are you?' and
with that my daughter woke up in bed and said 'hey you,'
and he got panicky and ran downstairs." She could not say
if the accused was the man she saw, though he lived next
door to her.

The defendant said in a statement that he had not been
in the woman's house for years. He was drunk that night
and had gone straight to bed. Forensic experts then produced in court articles from the house which bore the
defendant's fingerprints.

Justice Good congratulated the experts on their "con-
clusive testimony" and sentenced the boy to 12 months
in prison. He appeared in the next case also, with two
other young men. "I looked in the window of the chemist's shop and saw three male figures. They came to the
front of the shop and I saw them sharing out medical
preparations. They broke in for the purpose of taking
drugs," the garda said.

The first defendant had a conviction for housebreaking
and larceny for which he was fined, in 1970. He was
currently appealing a sentence for the larceny of drugs,
imposed on him in February of this year. The second
defendant had three convictions for larceny and receiving,
for which he had served two six-month jail terms. Last
year he served nine months for larceny of drugs. The
third defendant was at this stage asleep.

The F.L.A.C. barrister for the first defendant said that
his client was a registered drug-addict at Jervis Street
Hospital. He had been a registered out-patient there for
twelve months. "He is in a very bad way, Justice. He has
arranged to go into a drug-centre to stay for recuperation.
On the night in question here, he was drunk."

"He has convictions dating back to . . ." began the
justice. "You can see from his demeanour that he is
in a bad way, Justice," said the barrister, "and he is prepared to be 'washed out,' as he says himself. He has been
working for a month now, and he has a wife and two
children. He is pleading for the mercy of this court,
in fact. Perhaps it's lucky that he was caught, because

now we may be able to impose discipline on him. If the sentence is suspended I think he will do quite well, later on."

"I haven't been given a chance," this defendant said. "Every time the drug-squad see me, they pull me in. I didn't want to go back to prison. It gets on me nerves. On the night I was caught we didn't know what we were doing."

"Do justice to yourself," said Justice Good. "Are you seriously telling me you didn't know what you were doing?"

"We couldn't reason with ourselves, we were so drunk. Pain-killers get you out of your head — they make you high — I don't remember what happened that night. I'm earning £24 a week now. Jervis Street give me stuff to keep me calm and away from drugs."

Said the justice: "The fact that they were stealing drugs, in my opinion, does not take away from the offence of breaking and entering other people's premises. I've had to deal with numerous drug cases, and I've always tried hard to show leniency, where a man could possibly be treated and rehabilitated to normal life. I like to help drug addicts. I believe they could be helped but when it comes to the committing of a crime of breaking and entering premises, I'm not going to show a lenient hand.

"Here we have men with previous convictions, not just in drugs, but of breaking and entering. They think any man can come here and say 'I'm on drugs' as if that were an excuse. House-breaking and larceny is on the increase, and the sooner something is done to stop it, the better. Nine months each."

The sleeping boy woke up. "Can it run in with my twelve?" he asked.

Chapter 4
Home Life

"This assault happened after severe provocation. It may be necessary to go into the whole long story of marital history, and I think you should know that, before the case begins," the husband's solicitor told District Justice Good in Dublin District Court 4. The Justice looked at the clock. It was twenty-five to four. "We're dealing with an assault," he said shortly. The courts are supposed to rise at four o'clock.

A doctor who had examined the wife the morning after gave evidence. "I'll be brief," he said. "I found abrasions to the left side of her head and the left side of her jaw. There were bruise marks on her left breast and severe bruising on her left forearm, thigh and shin. She was very agitated and upset." The doctor added that she was 16 weeks pregnant at the time, and he gave her some sedation.

The wife, young, fresh, neat and from the country, took the stand. Her husband, young, fresh, neat and from the same part of the country, listened impassively to her from his seat in the dock.

"Things had been bad like, between us, and we weren't talking that night," she said. "I came home and he was in bed. I was nervous about being alone in the house with him because he has assaulted me before. My sisters were going away home for Easter and I was thinking of going with them. He had already been stopping out all night and that kind of thing. When he came in, and I'd ask him where he'd been, he beat me.

"He was in bed that night, it was about eight o'clock, and I didn't wake him. I decided to go out with my sister. I went and she wasn't there, so I came home again. Then I decided to go and look for my other sister. I left a note for him, saying that I had spent the money he gave me, £20.

"He had given it to me the day before, and I hadn't spent it at all. I told him that because I wanted the money for going home. I went out to find my other sister, and she wasn't in either. I came home and he wasn't in. He had gone out, to the pub, I suppose, because it's the only place he ever goes. I went to bed, as I was very tired and had been working all day. Next thing I remember I was caught by the hair and dragged out of bed. He started speaking and I knew it was him. He asked me why I had locked the front door and I said I hadn't, and he said he had to put his fist through the window and would need 20 stitches in his hand.

"He started kicking me in the stomach . . . yes, he knew I was pregnant . . . and he kept on kicking me, and I asked him to let me go downstairs to the bathroom, and I told him I was having a miscarriage, thinking, that way he'd let me go. I was folded over in pain at this stage. I went to go downstairs and he gave me a kick on the way down, saying, 'O.K., if that's what you want.' I got to the bathroom and he put his foot in, to open the door.

"I sat on the toilet with my head down and he kept talking and gave me a kick in the mouth. Then he went to the drawer and got a little sharp steak knife. He said, 'I intended when I got in tonight to kill you and I think that's what I'll do.' I screamed and I think that frightened him. He dropped the knife and said, 'Ah, you're not worth it.'

"Then he asked me where the bottle opener was, and I didn't know, and he went and got it, and came back and opened a small bottle of beer. He took one drink out of it and poured the rest down on top of me and then hit me with the bottle. Then he went up to the sitting room and called me up and started beating me again, kicking me in the stomach. He stubbed out cigarettes on my face and nose. He carried on kicking me, trying to get me in the stomach and I put my left arm down to protect myself, and he kicked my arm instead. Then he caught me by the hair of the head and told me to look at the door he had to break in. We'd both had trouble with the lock; you have to know how to twist the key. I put up my hand to show him and he said, 'Don't you dare.' He thought I was trying to get out. He started kicking and shouting and I wasn't able for any more. He sat me on one chair and he sat on the other and started saying rude things to me . . . .

"Well, if I didn't answer he would slap me — and would say, 'You're a prostitute. What are you?' and I'd have to answer, 'I'm a prostitute', and he'd go on with those sort of things. He asked me where was the note I'd left and I hadn't a clue, and he told me not to come to bed till I'd found the note, and that I was lucky he hadn't killed me as he intended to. He told me if I was thinking of running away in the morning, it wouldn't be advisable.

"Later I crept up to bed, and then I crept down again, with my clothes, and I dressed myself and lay down on the sofa. He came down and brought me back to bed. It was near morning by that time. Later I said I wanted to go down and make a cup of tea, and he let me, and I put on the kettle to make him think I was making tea, and I went round to my sister and then to the guards. The doctor told me to go home for a rest, and I went down there for a long time . . .

"Yes, I saw my husband a few times before the baby was born. I'd come up for a week or so, but it didn't work out. He came down home too, but he assaulted me there as well, once outside my parents' home."

She told of one occasion when she went to his home in the country for the night, and accompanied him next day to the Galway races, because she was afraid to leave him. "I knew if I did that, I'd have had it." After the races they went to a pub, and she pretended to go to the toilet, but instead escaped in a taxi. He followed her home, and beat her outside the front door, and said he'd "swing" for any member of her family that interfered.

In cross-examination by the husband's solicitor she said that she had gone back to him several times in the hope of making the marriage work. He had occasionally sent her £9 a week maintenance, as awarded by a court. After the birth of their daughter, she had gone back to him, using money she had got in presents. He at that time was out of work.

When her money started running out, after a week, and the rent was due, he had said to her that if he had to starve, she could starve too. She left him then. He was still beating her. Then she went to Wales to join her sister.

She admitted to the solicitor that she had once spent £30 in one afternoon on one-armed bandits in an amusement arcade. She said that when she had left the note about having spent the £20 "again" he might have interpreted this to mean that she had gambled it away. She also admitted that the night before the case was heard, when she had come back from Wales, she had met her husband, gone dancing with him, had a meal afterwards, and then sat up most of the night talking.

"Isn't that a strange way to behave towards a man you're about to have committed to prison?" asked the solicitor. She burst into tears. "I pity him," she said, "and he had no money".

She denied that she had always intended to leave him, although within two days of rejoining him, after the birth of the baby, she had removed her English medical card from their box of effects. She denied that she had often lost amounts gambling on one-armed bandits. The trouble, she said, was that he'd go to work, get an idea in his head, think about it all day and then come home and accuse her.

No, she wasn't a nag, though the solicitor later produced a next door neighbour who testified that one night he had heard a woman's voice talking, talking, talking all night, without a cheep being heard from the man. She denied that she wanted him committed to prison. "If things were right, I'd want to live with him," she burst into tears again.

The solicitor called the husband to the stand. It was twenty past four. "I don't intend to sit late. I don't know what you intend to do," said the Justice.

The husband was a prison officer at the time of the assault. The solicitor said he was retarded for his age, with severe problems of immaturity. He had since resigned from the prison service. The husband spoke quietly. He admitted the assault, but couldn't remember the details. He thought he had slapped her once, while she was smoking, and that might have caused the cigarette burns.

"You knew she was pregnant?" asked the Justice angrily. "Yes, but I was in a terrible temper," he said, "and I was very sorry afterwards. I got into such a temper when she had locked the door."

The solicitor pointed out that the doctor had given no evidence of cigarette burns.

"I don't blame her if she says I wasn't good to her," said the husband. "I thought I was good to her, but she thinks I wasn't."

"How can you say you were good to her, when you assaulted her so savagely? A woman who was bearing your child?" asked the Justice.

He said that he was now earning £10 a week in a part time job, and had to pay £6 in rent for a flat. He hoped to get a job in a semi-State body.

The probation officer testified. "Both parties are very attached to each other," he said. "They periodically come together and then blow up. The trouble is his personality. He had an immature personality structure, which might perhaps mature with time. He is very easily frustrated and has severe psycho-sexual problems, which can erupt easily into violence. He is the type of man who wouldn't attack another man. I agree with the wife, that she is right to fear for the safety of the baby. My opinion is, that the only time I sleep happily is when they're apart . . . I wouldn't blame the wife. I think they love each other, but he has a nature which easily erupts. In close contact with another person, there is violence from him. He told me he didn't mind too much about her gambling, and I think myself it was her way of release from trouble, much the same way as another woman shoplifts in a cry for help . . . I would hope they never come together again, frankly."

The Justice said that nothing justified assault. He referred to the husband as "sub-human" and a "beast". He remanded the case to March, for one reason only — to see if the husband would maintain and support his wife and child. If he didn't, he wouldn't "be out of the woods". He'd be in prison.

12 December 1974

A sad and tragic case

I remembered them from somewhere. He had dark eyes and clean clothes, and his voice was soft, as he stood before District Justice Ua Donnchadha in Dublin Court No. 6. His wife clung, timid and vulnerable, to the social worker. She had a bruised and blackened eye.

The social worker gave evidence: "Mr. Smith asked me if he could see his wife. He would not accept that she was not willing to see him again. She did agree, but she refused to see him alone, and I was present at the meeting, with a nun from the convalescent home.

"He became angry, abusive and threatening when she said she didn't want to see him any more, and he said that if he did see her again, he would cut her head off, even if he swung for it. He started to leave the room and then came back and punched her with his clenched fist. She bled profusely and her face swelled."

The wife told the district justice that she had been operated on last year for a severe brain haemorrhage.

The husband agreed with the evidence. "The testimony is basically true," he said. "I did go out to the convent to meet my wife. I was hoping for a reconciliation or, at least, for some narrowing of the gulf between us. I did assault my wife and make those threats, though I'd like to say that they were made in the heat of the moment and there was no possibility of following them through.

"I have had a year of considerable stress, worry and frustration, and my wife has been wandering away for days, weeks, months, away from our home. I believe this to be a result of the surgery my wife underwent. She suffered a complete change of personality after it,

53

and it was a harrowing time for me. We have five children, the eldest six years, the youngest six months. They're at the moment being cared for in a home attached to the convalescent centre."

He was currently unemployed, he said. "I have had a number of jobs in the past," he continued, "but I am unskilled. My last steady job was with Dublin Corporation last year, but they let me go in the autumn. I had a job after that, lasting two days."

He was currently drawing the single man's unemployment benefit of £4.35 a week; the social worker had arranged to have the other money paid to his wife and children.

Prior to the operation, he said, his relationship with his wife was "basically very good, though, of course, we had the odd row. I would like to say that the assault was completely unpremeditated, despicable though it was. It was just the circumstances of last year welled up, and spilled over. I'm terribly sorry. I'd like to apologise to my wife."

The social worker went into the witness box. "The children have been in the care of the Eastern Health Board since March, 1972. When I first met Mrs. Smith her condition was poor and she was in a state of exhaustion. Five of them lived in a room in Benburb Street. They were without money or food and the gas was cut off. Mr. Smith had been drinking heavily. Relations between him and his wife were good, and they were good to their children.

"In February, 1972, she had a cerebral haemorrhage and was in hospital for several months, followed by a long period of convalescence. Mr. Smith made a big effort to look after his children then, but was unsuccessful and we took them into care. No, there was no evidence of cruelty or anything. He asked us to have them until his wife was better.

"Since her illness, Mrs. Smith has felt unable to live with her husband for any length of time. She disappears. A child has been born since the operation. On one occasion she took the one-year-old child home with her for a trial period, but she left the home again. I found her in a distressed condition.

"In August, 1972, she finally left the home for good. She wanders about, at the mercy of the world looking for shelter. She says her husband beats her, ill-treats her, undermines her confidence in herself and treats her as though she were insane.

"He brought her to my office once. He had found her in St. Stephen's Green and he was unwilling to allow her to return home. I arranged accommodation for her in an institution. She was terrified of meeting him, though he persists in seeing her, and on one occasion had to be removed by the gardai. I think they are irreconcilable until she regains her stability."

The husband said that most of this story was true, but he denied that he beat his wife, or that he drank heavily. The wife said she wanted to live away from her husband "till we sort out something, get something fixed".

This was a very sad and tragic case, said District Justice Ua Donnchadha. He gave the husband a six-month suspended sentence, provided he kept the peace for a year and stayed away from his wife.

The wife and social worker went out of the court and the husband looked at me, and I remembered. In the office I looked up an interview I had done with them, in September, 1971, when they lived in Benburb Street, the hovels the Corporation provide for rent-defaulters. The room in which they existed was filled with a double bed and cot.

Here is an extract of what I wrote then: "They have only one real worry now. There wouldn't be room in the bed, or indeed the room, if there was another baby. 'It's not a question of religion,' said his wife. 'The priest said it wouldn't be fair on me to have another child, especially there. But the doctor said the pill wouldn't suit me. There's just the rhythm method, if you can keep track of the days in this room. But one day's just like another here. . .'

"John said: 'I suppose you could call it shock treatment. The way I see it is, I'm up to my eyes at the moment. I am determined not to sink any further. I'll soon be out of here; soon as I get a job. Maybe they'll evict me then to Ballsbridge. . . the kids are underfoot all the time, and they have to play, don't they?'

" 'You sit here at night, with the wife, just the two of us, and the walls are all about and the light shines on the kids in the bed . . . And if I go to the pub, I'm laughing in my pint, and then the wife's face comes up, and I think of her back here. We did get out together one night, and it cheered her up for two whole days . . .

" 'It was difficult in Ballymun, you see, between the work and the dole and the arrears. Immediately you got a job, the rent went up, but you'd work a lying week, and then you'd borrow money to see you through the fortnight, but by the time you'd paid that off, the rent had built up and it went on and on. Plus you'd have the kids to feed, and gas and electricity . . .

" 'Times I was bewildered and then we gave up trying. We got several warning notices from the Corporation. Suddenly there was 24 hours left. A social worker got us this place in Benburb Street . . .

" 'One thing I regret. My old man was retired out of the British Army, and they offered to send me to school in England for two years. I wouldn't go.

" 'I might have been a doctor by now, a respected member of society. On the other hand, I wouldn't have met my wife . . .

" ' I know if a man doesn't pay his rent, he should be punished. I mean, you can't just let him live rent-free, and his standards would have to be lowered a lot. But, in this case, they seem to have lowered the boom. Not on me, I can take it, but on the wife and the children. It's sins of the fathers, I suppose. Then, again, they'll tell you it's no sin to be unemployed. There's something wrong somewhere. I just can't put my finger on it . . .'"

Five months later, his wife haemorrhaged. Then she got pregnant. Her children were taken into care. She left her husband and wandered the streets, "at the mercy of the world". He met her, he hit her, they ended up in court.

There's something wrong somewhere. The court couldn't

help.

Put him down, guard

The travelling woman came into Dublin District Court No. 4 and called something and was ushered out. Several times in the course of the afternoon she wandered in and was quickly removed. They let her stay during the final case, when her husband appeared before District Justice Ó hUadhaigh.

He had been drinking, obviously, and was also distressed as they brought him up from the cells. As the court guard began his evidence the man interrupted. The garda continued talking as the man said: "My child shouldn't be in Mountjoy. She should be in the convent."

"In reply," finished the guard, "he said 'I was found drunk in the courthouse looking for me child'."

"Are you guilty or not guilty?", asked the Justice.

"I'm guilty of looking for me own child. She shouldn't be in Mountjoy Jail. She's only 13," the man said.

"Were you drunk here in court today?", asked the Justice. "I was drunk, all right, I don't deny it. Sure me childer has me tormented," said the man. "What's your trouble?", asked the Justice. "I'm in a bad way about me childer," the man said. "One is in Birmingham, one is in the convent, and another is in Mountjoy. The one in the convent is fit for Mountjoy. She could take it. But the one in Mountjoy now is not fit for it. She's not fit for jail. There's me child's photo," he said, taking it from his wife, who had reached into her shawl.

They smiled at it together and offered it up to the Justice on his cushioned chair behind the bench above. "But why are you drunk?" asked the Justice. "For me childer, I'm drunk over me childer," said the man. "That's nonsense. Drink doesn't help," said the Justice. He leant over his bench and said to the court clerk: "He's near the crying stage." Then he looked at the photo and said: "Isn't his boy a cripple?" "Aahhh," said the man. "Watch it," said the Justice to the clerk, he'll be crying in a minute. "That's my eldest son," said the man, tears in his eyes, "and isn't it no wonder for me to be worried?". "He broke his back in Wales," said the wife. "And he has a colour camera and all," said the Justice, holding up the photo. "Well, it's £2, or one month in jail. Have you £2 on you?". "Sure you know I haven't two and a half pence," said the man. "That's too bad. One month in Mountjoy," said the Justice.

"What about my child?", called the man as they led him down the stairs to the cells. "Hey, my child shouldn't be in Mountjoy. She's too young. She's not fit for it." "Put him down, guard," said the Justice, and he rose from his bench and the court closed.

Outside the wife hurried round to the wall of the Bridewell. From the cell above her daughter reached her hands out the broken barred window. She wanted cigarettes. There was another travelling girl with her, who had been granted bail, on her mother's surety, but she refused to leave the jail. She wanted to keep the other girl company. "It'll only be till Thursday, ma," she called to her mother standing below with a young son. This woman turned round to the wife and asked her how she had got on. "Ah, it's £2 or a month," she said, "and we didn't have it." They told me that the wife's young child had been drowned earlier this year. They'd all be back on Thursday to see how the childer got on.

"Put him down, guard," said the Justice.

8 November 1973

Under age

From Dublin District Court Number 4, we could hear the screaming. Something was happening in Court 6. The screaming continued down into the cells. I went round to Court 6 and saw a man in the hallway arguing with an inspector. "I want the name and number of that guard who took those children down the steps", the man was saying.

The inspector refused to give the name. He gave his own, though. Later, in the courtyard, the inspector and the man continued the argument.

"You would be doing the country a far better service if you helped the justice", the inspector was shouting.

I discovered that they were arguing about the two itinerant girls about whom I wrote yesterday. They had been held in custody since Monday on a charge of breaking and entering and stealing clothes from a boutique.

The two girls appeared yesterday morning before District Justice Good, and were convicted. The justice remanded them, pending a probation officer's report. There were screams and scuffles, and they were removed to the cells below for an hour. With 20 minutes they were brought back up and one of the girls, her arms covered in cuts, threatened to commit suicide. She knocked over a microphone and tried to bang her head on the bench.

The justice passed sentence of six months on one girl, who informed him that he had no right to sentence her as she was only 14. The justice, after consultation with the clerks, said that he was not satisfied as to the ages of the girls and remanded them to the Children's Court whence they were immediately conveyed. There it was ascertained that their ages were 14 and 15, and they were given the Probation Act.

Their parents were not present in any of the courts. The girls were last seen, in the words of the court official to me, "screaming abuse and running down the street".

9 November 1973

Motherhood

She was 15 years old and she was arrested, drunk in charge of her child, in the early hours of Saturday, February 15th. She was released in her own bail from the District Court that morning, because of uncertainty about her age. That night, towards 10 o'clock, she was drunk in charge of her child again. She was arrested, lodged in Mountjoy Jail, and remanded in custody there from the Children's Court. The child was taken to a hospital. On

Wednesday, February 26th, she was released from jail following a High Court decision that jail is an illegal place of detention for minors.

Which, of course, adult jails are. But, of course, this State has not yet, despite repeated demands over the years, provided proper custodial places for minors in need of care.

Yesterday morning, February 27th, the 15-year-old girl turned up in court, of her own volition, to answer multiple charges.

The Eastern Health Board brought along her six-week-old baby. Her other year-old baby is already in care, in an institution which the girl voluntarily brought the baby to because she could not cope with two children.

The State withdrew some of the multiple charges, and the girl faced only two; that she unlawfully abandoned her child in such a manner that its life and health were likely to be injured; and that later she had been drunk in charge of her child. The defence barrister made the opening point that the latter charge had only that morning been pressed against her and that they had not had time to prepare an adequate defence.

"I saw her sitting in a doorway leaning over to her right", the prosecuting guard told District Justice Kennedy in the Dublin Children's Court. "When we lifted her up the child was underneath, wrapped in a blanket. She was fairly drunk. The blanket was wet. The child was cold and wet". It was difficult to say he said, if the blanket was wet due entirely to urine from the baby.

"Was the rug wet all over?", asked the Justice. It was, said the guard.

Was the child any differently dressed than children of the other travelling people, considering the poor circumstances under which they lived, asked the barrister. "Possibly not", said the guard. "She told me she was 15 and unmarried and that she had put her other baby into a home".

A doctor from the hospital where the baby was lodged gave evidence. "The child was wet, cold and hungry. There was a strong smell of urine off it. It was filthy dirty. It was not, however, undernourished. There were sores on both knees, on the right big toe, and the left forearm." He agreed with the barrister that the sores did not result from beating or deliberate ill-treatment.

He further agreed that the child was reasonably well-dressed. "If the baby was in fact exposed, would its health have been put at risk because of its clothing?", asked the barrister.

"No, not at risk from the cold", said the doctor.

"Did the child appear to be ill-treated?", asked the barrister.

"No, it wasn't in fact ill-treated as such", said the doctor. The barrister suggested to the Justice that the child was not exposed as such, in the language of the charge, and that there had been no attempt on the part of the girl to abandon it. The Justice would not dismiss the charge. The barrister put the girl in the witness box.

"Did you expose the child in any way that night?" asked the barrister. "No", she said. "Did you have drink taken?", asked the barrister. "I had, just a little", she said. "Did you think the health or life of the child was likely to be endangerd?", asked the barrister. "No", she said.

She had left the baby earlier with her sister-in-law, she said, and had collected it later.

"Where was the baby when you went for it?", asked the Justice.

"In my sister-in-law's arms", she replied.

The Justice dismissed the charge.

Another guard gave evidence on the second charge.

"At approximately 1.45 a.m. (20 hours previous to the first charge) I found the defendant sitting in the middle of the road with a child in her arms. Traffic coming from both directions was stopped". Following arrest and charge, the girl had replied, "I am sorry for being drunk".

The barrister made a technical point, which was rejected, and he said he would not go into further evidence. "I would only say that the fact that she was not provided with a copy of the charge sheet until this hearing began did not help us to prepare a case", he said.

The Justice convicted her and fined her £1, with seven

days to pay, seven days' imprisonment in default.

The prosecution then applied for an order under the Fit Persons Act to have the baby taken into care.

The first guard returned to the stand to say that he had visited the home address given by the girl, a derelict house in the city-centre, where her family and relatives lived.

"It was no place for any human being", he said. "She says she lives there. I wouldn't let a dog live in it." (He was right. I have often visited the place, on request from the girl's mother, who is looking for a Corporation home — unsuccessfully).

"Can you say whether the father of the child will take responsibility for it?", asked the barrister.

"I can't say", said the guard. "I don't know whether the father is around or not". The father, who was sitting in court beside me, became very agitated. He was 26. "Can I not talk?", the father whispered to me. "She is not able to. She doesn't know these big words. I was down the country when this happened. She lives with me out in the caravan".

"The girl did not ask me, after she had been in for two days, how her baby was", the guard was continuing. "Today, when the baby was brought to court, she did not even look at it".

The barrister put the girl back on the witness stand.

"Would you like to keep your baby?", he asked her. "I want the two of them", she said. "Are you in receipt of the unmarried mother's allowance?", asked the barrister. "No", she said. "Are you in receipt of the children's allowance?", asked the barrister. "No", she said. "I went down for the children's allowance, and they told me to come back for it when I was 16." "Did they give you any information about home assistance?", asked the barrister. "They told me to go another place, for money, and I went there and they told me to go to another place, out in Phibsboro, and I didn't go anymore", she said. "I don't know whether this is relevant," said the barrister, "but were you given any advice by the hospital or anyone, after the birth of the first child, on how to prevent having another child?" "No", she said. The barrister asked her if she intended to get married. She did, she said.

The barrister asked the Justice if it would be of any assistance to call the father of the two babies.

"Not much, I'd say", said the Justice.

The father became quietly agitated again. "I have £400 of property", he whispered to me. "Are they going to put her in jail? Are they taking the baby? Can I not speak? She doesn't understand."

"I'm not going to commit this child formally into custody as such", said the Justice. "I won't send it to an industrial school. I'm making an order under the Fit Persons Act directing the child to be taken into care. If she gets married, they may get the child back, if they get into a house or something like that".

"I wonder, in the circumstances if that section of the Constitution relating to the State and its duty to the family unit is relevant?" asked the barrister desperately.

"This is not a constitutional court", said the Justice. "You make a reference here to the State not making an effort to advise this girl. She is a member of the itinerant class. There is a very active section of the Social Work Department attached to this class, and I am sure she could get all the advice she needs there."

(There is, in fact, a very active section. Three social workers looking after 450 families of the travelling people in Dublin and county. Active is not necessarily sufficient).

She advised the barrister that they could make application for the return of the child to parental custody at any time in the future. The case closed.

Off went the baby with the Health Board. Out into the street went the girl and the father of her children. No recommendation was made in court that the girl be given formal assistance with her problems. The girl, like her baby, is a child in the eyes of the law. All she got out of the last two weeks was a £1 fine, two weeks in Mountjoy Jail, and the loss of her baby.

What in the name of God does the Children's Court exist for? To put children into jail and take pound notes off them?

28 February 1975

Chapter 5
Women

What would you have done? The heart has its reasons, but the law must have its course. She was nearly 40 and her sister was in trouble, and District Justice Good presided in Dublin District Court 6.

She had been a book-keeper for one of the biggest firms in Ireland, her solicitor told the justice. They collected rents from over 4,000 houses, and for her responsibilities she was paid £17 a week nett. Two years ago, the marriage of her sister ran into difficulties. Her husband left her, and there were children to support. The defendant decided to help the sister out, by sending her money.

She issued receipts for rent money, kept the monies, and did not enter the amounts into the corresponding ledger. Her sister benefitted. Then she was found out. She confessed all, and pleaded guilty. A remand was granted. During the period of remand, the defendant sold her house and paid back the amount due to her employers, a sum totalling nearly £1,000 over a two-year period.

Now she stood before the justice, a "single woman", as her defence solicitor pleaded, without a home, and without a job — she had been sacked who had done this thing in order to help her married sister. Just before her deeds had been discovered, the firm had raised her salary to £1,800 a year. Too late. She would be 40 in November, the solicitor urged.

"You were employed for nine years in a position of trust," the justice said. "Do you realise that you betrayed that trust? Isn't that so? When did it strike you — when did your conscience first trouble you? When did you realise that it was wrong?"

"I knew all along that it was wrong," she said.

"Yes, but when did your conscience trouble you?" asked the justice, who apparently distinguished between legal and moral wrong.

"I had hoped to pay the money back before it came to light," she said.

"The sad feature is, that this was a very responsible job," said the justice sadly. "Of course, the more responsible a job is, the more trust is expected of the employee. In the ordinary way, one should inflict serious punishment on anyone who betrays the trust of an employer." (Can an employer betray trust by paying a miserable wage? The justice did not discuss this.) "You had misfortunes, and you were anxious to help out your family, but that is not in any way an excuse," continued the justice, who did not hold family distress as an excuse for breaking the law. "You impressed me as a good type of young lady, who had the misfortune to be tempted and fall," he continued biblically. "You're obviously a lady of good character and some education, and good upbringing, and full of remorse, and I'll impose a 12 months' sentence, suspended for 12 months."

And away went the lady of good character, and previously unblemished record, who had lost her job and her home through helping her married sister.

18 September 1974

In view of the circumstances

She had the slacks concealed under her coat and was heading for the door when she was detained by the store security guard, the ban garda told District Justice Good in Dublin District Court 4. The woman was pleading guilty to the charge. Her solicitor however was not in court, the ban garda finished.

"Well, perhaps we may be able to dispose of it anyway", the justice said quietly. "Has she any record?" She had four previous convictions, the ban garda said. "Four previous convictions? For the same type of thing? Shop-lifting?" asked the justice, his voice raising, his face changing.

For the same type of thing, agreed the ban-garda. The woman was married and expecting her 14th child. Her husband was unemployed.

"Fourteen children", said the justice, looking down at the woman. She pulled her coat nervously around her swollen belly. "Well, what do you have to say for yourself? This is the fourth, no fifth offence of shop-lifting", continued the justice.

"The last time was for my children", whispered the woman.

"I beg your pardon?" asked the justice.

"And this time my husband was getting a chance of a job", continued the woman. "He's been idle this two years, and I was trying to steal a pair of overalls to make him presentable".

"But this is your fifth offence", said the justice.

"The other times it was for my children", said the woman.

"You've certainly brought a lot of children into the world. Fourteen", said the justice.

"Thirteen", said the woman, "I'm expecting the 14th".

"You present a problem to me", said the justice.

"I owe £100 rent and the light's about to be cut off", said the woman, crying now.

"Does your husband know?" asked the justice.

"No", she said, "he doesn't know about any of them. I get belted around for less".

"You mean if he knew, there'd be trouble", translated the justice. "What does he work at?"

"Any kind of work", she said, still crying. "A couple of months ago he got three days' work and — ".

"You look young. How old are your children?" interrupted the justice.

"The eldest is 15 and the youngest is 12 months",

said the woman.

"You know, this is your fifth offence. What am I going to do with you? Can you help me out yourself? You're going to have another child shortly", said the justice.

"You'd do anything when your children are hungry", whispered the woman.

"I know that. Are you short of money?" the justice asked this pregnant mother of thirteen, whose husband was unemployed.

"I owe £100 in rent", the woman said.

"What happened on the four previous occasions?" the justice turned to the ban garda.

"She appealed and got the three months' sentence suspended", said the ban garda.

"You see, you've been given a chance", said the justice.

"No, justice, I was never given a chance. I was always sentenced", she said.

"Yes, but you got out on appeal, didn't you?" countered the justice. "I really don't know what to do with you. When are you expecting the baby?".

"The end of March", she said.

"I think I must get rid of this case today", said the justice. "If it's hanging over your head it's not going to do you any good. You have me worried as to what I should do with you in your condition. It looks to me as if you have a lot of money troubles. I can well imagine you have trouble looking after 14 children. But you really can't go on stealing".

"It's just that . . . I don't know . . . ", she said, burying her face in her hands.

"If I give you a chance, a suspended sentence? In view of the circumstances? It's a rather pathetic case", said the justice. "But ultimately one has to cry halt. You can't go on indefinitely stealing from a shop. I'll impose a suspended sentence.

"Now promise me you'll keep out of trouble. If you steal you'll have to be punished. I don't want to take a mother away from her children, but you're forcing my hand. You're not helping me. Do you promise not to steal any more?"

"I promise", she said.

"Three months' suspended sentence", pronounced the justice.

Had the woman's solicitor represented her, he might or might not have told the justice how she squatted into a two-bedroom Corporation flat from a one-bedroom Corporation flat; how her previous home had been destroyed by fire; how she suffered from anaemia. And other details.

It might or might not have made a difference.

23 January 1974

The fight against crime

It was from a legal point of view, a straight allegation of shoplifting before District Justice Ó hUadhaigh in Dublin District Court 6. The woman had paid for the meat and the oranges, the store detective said but she had not paid for another package of meat, which was concealed under the lettuce, beside the cauliflower.

The woman rose on her own defence. "It's only a little bag, your honour," she said, holding up a shopping bag which was decorated with many holes. "You can see yourself it's wide open. You could see anything through it."

She had no receipt for the groceries," the store detective said. "I checked with the roll on the cash register and there was no amount registered for twenty and one half-pence of mince meat."

"I didn't go in to take any meat," the woman said.

"I accept that you didn't go in to take any," the justice said, "but you did take it."

"I didn't even know it was there until she showed it to me under the lettuce," the woman said.

The store manager was called to testify that the store did exist and was properly registered. The justice asked the woman if she wished to cross-examine him.

"Sure I never seen him before in my life," the woman said.

The justice asked her if she had anything to say on her own behalf.

"There's nothing I can say, sir," said the woman.

"Hold your hand," said the justice and he advised her as to her rights. "Now what do you want to do?", he asked her. "I don't mind what I do," she said, "because I didn't steal anything."

"I went into the store," she continued, "because I wanted to buy two yoghourts. But they'd gone up. They were fivepence each two days ago and now they are 7½ pence each. So I didn't bother. I bought meat and two oranges."

"That's called inflation," said the justice. "But you bought stuff anyway. There's four or five articles in that shopping bag." "I bought this packet of toffees for my grandchildren at fivepence," said the woman. "I always buy this kind. Then I bought the meat and the oranges."

"What about the meat you didn't pay for?", asked the justice. "Well, the girl there found the meat and I didn't know anything about it," the woman said. "Anything more I don't know about," she said, "and as for the rest," she continued, bringing the articles one by one out of her shopping bag, "I bought the lettuce in Moore Street, you can get two for tenpence there, and the cauliflower only costs ten pence there. They are much dearer in the store." "The store has to pay staff and overheads," said the justice. (I thought stores put small shopkeepers out of business because they bought and sold in bulk?) "Anyway, there's a strange atmosphere about all this," continued the justice, "and I'm convicting you."

"Oh Lord, I was never in court in my life," said the woman.

"Probation of Offenders Act," said the justice, "and the meat restored to the owners."

"I'll pay for the meat," said the woman.

"Why would you pay for it if you didn't want it?", asked the justice. "Probation Act. Away with you."

27 June 1975

Aren't I well, mammy?

"I remanded this woman for a psychiatric report which the prison has not yet been able to furnish," said District Justice Ua Donnchadha in Dublin District Court No. 4. He asked the woman if anyone was representing her. "I don't know. I wrote in for legal aid," she said. "Yes, I saw the application for the first time this morning," said the Justice. "I don't want to be detained," said the woman, agitating on the edge of the bench. She was charged with shoplifting.

She wore a black coat over a denim suit. Her face was made-up. She was neat and modern. Her hands, thick-fingered and red, had known work. The Justice asked her if she had any relatives in court. She indicated her mother, an old woman, seated against the wall. The Justice turned to the guard and said: "You asked for this girl to be re-manded, didn't you?"

"No sir, I didn't ask," said the guard. "She appeared to be in a distressed condition in court and you suggested the psychiatric report."

"I don't want to be remanded in custody. I had drink taken," said the woman, starting to her feet. A court guard, there to watch prisoners in the dock, shushed her and sat her down. He pointed silently to the Justice, who was calling the mother into the witness box.

"She's deaf," said the woman. "Is this your daughter?" asked the Justice. "Yes," said the mother. "Yes, I am," said the woman. The guard shushed her.

"How old is she?" asked the Justice.

"Thirty-six," said the mother.

"I'm not 36, mammy, I'm 26," called the woman. The guard shushed her. "She works in the factory and lives with me. I'm a widow woman. My husband died on March 3rd," said the mother.

"I was satisfied on her last appearance here that your daughter didn't comprehend what was going on around her," said the Justice.

"I can't hear you. What did you say?" the old woman said, craning her head.

"Was your daughter ever in hospital?" shouted the Justice.

"Oh she was, with nerves and excitement," said the mother.

"My father was knocked down," said the woman. The guard shushed her.

"She was treated for a long time," said the mother.

"It was only six weeks, mammy," said the woman. The guard shushed her.

"How long ago?" asked the Justice.

"Five years ago," said the mother.

The woman called, "Mammy." The guard shushed her. "Keep quiet," admonished the Justice.

The woman turned to the guard, now seated beside her, his hand on her arm. "Will he let me go?" she asked. He shushed her.

"I want a psychiatric report on her," said the Justice to the mother.

"I'd agree to her being treated," said the mother.

"No, mammy, no, I'll be detained. You don't understand. If I get treatment I'll be detained. Mammy, if you say that I'll be detained," cried the woman. The guard shushed her and then stood up and back, away from her.

"I feel I must have a psychiatric report. I'm not satisfied your daughter fully comprehends her situation," said the Justice.

"I beg your pardon? I can't hear," said the mother.

"Aren't I well, mammy?" called the woman. "Please, mammy, tell them I'm well. I don't want to be detained. Tell them or I'll be detained." The guard shushed her.

"There are two ways I can get a psychiatric report," said the Justice to the mother.

"Pardon?" asked the mother.

"Am I any trouble to you mammy?" called the woman. The guard shushed her.

"You tell her what I'm saying," said the Justice to the clerk, who went and stood beside the mother. "Tell her," said the Justice, "that there are two ways I can get a report. One is through the medical officer in the prison and the other is if this lady can be taken by her to the psychiatrist on Usher's Island."

The clerk repeated the Justice's words . . . "and the second way is if she goes to Usher's Island of her own volition. Will you go guarantor for her that she will go there?"

"Yes," said the mother. The Justice asked her again if she was prepared to take her daughter to a psychiatrist.

"Where will I get him?" asked the mother.

"This gentleman here will explain," said the Justice, pointing to the probation officer. "I'll remand your daughter for one week."

"Am I on bail?" the woman asked the guard. He shushed her.

The Justice addressed the daughter. The guard indicated to her that she should stand during the address. She stood. She nodded. As she went out the door she took cigarettes out of her pocket.

Later they came back into court to acknowledge their signatures on the bail bond. The woman was smiling. She was not detained. She helped her mother down the court steps.

6 December 1973

Impulse

She would not have stood out in the Christmas crowd. She was about 55 and wore a raincoat, scarf and flat shoes. On her finger the wedding ring, in her hand the shopping bag, on her face the quiet trace of powder and lipstick. There are many who look just like her, even to the puzzled fear on her face as she stood in Dublin District Court 4 for the first time, before District Justice Ó hUadhaigh.

She had already spent some time in the cells below.

"In reply, she said 'I did take them,' and she signed the statement, justice," the ban-garda said. "She had £50 in her purse and she said that the baby's suit was for her grandchild. The suit and sweater were valued at £3.32."

"Are you a widow, madam?" asked the justice.

She was not.

"Why'd you do it?" asked the justice.

"I don't know. I just did it on impulse," she said softly.

"Impulse?" echoed the justice. "What's your husband's occupation?"

He was a porter.

"Well, you weren't pushed for money or anything," said the justice. "I don't know. Well, I mean, a baby's suit. Why'd the impulse hit when you were going for the sweater? Were they on different floors?"

The suit was downstairs and the sweater was upstairs, said the ban-garda.

"It took your impulse a long time to wear off," said the justice. "There's no such thing — well, we all have impulses, but we're not supposed to give in to them. There's no use telling me it was an impulse. You went on up the stairs and took a gansey. Have you ever gone bail here for anyone?"

She hadn't.

"It's remarkable," said the justice, "the number of people passing through here who all look alike. I don't know what I'm going to do with you . . . well, three months' imprisonment, suspended for a period of 12 months."

The justice wrote for a while on the charge sheet. "Ah sure this is all nonsense," he said then: "Three months' imprisonment, and that's the end of it."

The ban-garda and the big guard led the woman down the stairs. "Look, missus," called the justice after her, "if you'd whipped the child's suit and walked out, but you took something else . . ."

But the woman was already being led down, gently, between the supportive officers. At the bottom of the stairs, when it hit her, the whimpering began.

18 December 1973

Chapter 6
Children

There is no excuse for it. No reasonable, sane, sensible person could have sanctioned it. No Government Department can justify it. The closest approximation one can give to its effect is the last scene in the Hitchcock horror film "Psycho," when Anthony Perkins could be seen, through a spy-hole, huddled into himself in the corner of a solitary cell.

I am talking about the detention room at the unlit end of the downstairs corridor of Dublin Children's Court. I looked through the spy-hole yesterday morning at 10 minutes past noon. There was a metal grille covering the small hole in the door. You could not look through for too long, because of the draught that came coldly out from the room, forcing you to blink. If you were a child inside, you possibly could not look out at all, because the hole was too high up.

The colour scheme would have done a British Army interrogation centre proud. It is designed to dull, deaden and terrify. The high walls are painted, from floor to ceiling, a dark, deadly brown. Away up in the lofty ceiling a single bulb burns.

In that big, dark, empty brown room, there is one single item of furniture. A hard wooden bench, set against a bricked-up fireplace. It could seat four children. The other "captives" presumably stand. The floor is of stone. There are two narrow openings, each one foot deep, and three wide, cut into one wall just below the ceiling.

They are not windows because there is no glass. There are iron bars outside them, should any child take it into its head to leap 20 feet directly into the air, hang onto the ledge, and wriggle through.

Through these openings comes a little daylight, plus cold air and wind or rain. A woman in a fur coat, who had gone to visit her child in this detention room, came outside after 20 minutes, to try and warm up. She approached me at ten past twelve, crying, and asked me to come and look at her child, who had been incarcerated in that place since a quarter to eleven that morning, and who was condemned to wait until the Black Maria should arrive to take him away. (He hadn't been attending school, and the court took him in for care and attention and assessment. Oh God.)

I looked through the spy-hole and saw the child kicking his heels as he sat silently on the bench with another boy. They weren't talking. They were obviously cold. There was absolutely nothing for them to do, as they sat silently, coldly, in that high, bare, cold, dark brown room.

The woman led me to the toilets further down the corridor. The place was flooded. Deep puddles on the concrete floor. One toilet had no door. A piece of wood had been inserted into the jamb of the other door, which could not close, so that guards could keep watch on their captive children as they relieved themselves. There was not the customary encrusted faeces on the bowls of these court toilets. Presumably fear and embarrassment constipate the bowels.

Which is just as well, because there was no toilet paper. Naturally there were no seats on the toilets. A delph trough served as a sink. There was no soap or towel. In these dank confines do we keep our children, in the name of justice.

There is no excuse for it. There is a reason. Those responsible for it do not care. If they did, it wouldn't exist, would it?

27 September 1974

Criminal responsibility

The child squatted in the sunlight on the concrete slabs. He played with a magnet, picking up small pieces of iron, totally absorbed with his little feats. Across the courtyard tourists visited the State apartments of Dublin Castle. They were shown rich carpets and furnishings and paintings and invited to admire the Chinese vases and French period pieces. Here, they were told, the State entertained visiting foreign dignitaries.

At 2.30 p.m. the child got up and went through a door into the part of the Castle where the State prosecutes its children. He went upstairs and into a bare painted room, where cracks ran over the walls. Inserted into one large crack were two pieces of special glass. When the glass itself should finally crack, this will be an indication that the Children's Court is about to collapse.

The child stood under the mantel of the large fireplace set in against the side wall. In front of him, seated behind a raised wooden dais, sat District Justice Kennedy, flanked on either side by a probation officer and a court clerk. The prosecuting guard mounted the dais and sat on a chair and informed the justice that he had arrested the child, read out the charges to him in the station, cautioned him and had received no reply. He respectfully requested a remand.

The justice granted his request and informed the child of the date of his next court appearance. The next case was called. The child stood up under the mantel piece, his hands clasped behind his back. His brother whispered to him, from the public benches. The child looked round, came out of the fireplace, and left the court.

Children from the age of seven upwards are held criminally responsible for their actions in the Republic of Ireland.

11 September 1974

Bedtime story

The following story should not be true. But it is.

In Dublin City centre there is an adult holding prison. It is called the Bridewell and it is situated in the same yard as Dublin District Courts 4, 5, and 6. As you go through the iron gates, the Bridewell is on the left and the courts are on the right.

The Bridewell is used for holding overnight prisoners, who have been unable to get, or have been refused, station bail. It also holds prisoners brought down from Mountjoy Jail to stand trial that day in the courts. It also functions as a police station. Because the prisoners are not expected to spend a long time there, the Bridewell lacks even the minimum comforts, if you will excuse the term, of a regular prison.

Within the Bridewell, any day, you will meet a variety of people, accused of a variety of crimes, ranging from murder and rape, to drunkenness and petty theft. I say this as no comment on the people concerned. But it could be argued that some of these luckless people have become inured to the bonds that keep an average society together — bonds of kindness, or tolerance or desire not to harm others. For totally understandable reasons, people who have been forced by social conditions to commit anti-social acts, may not feel totally sociable towards others.

That is a problem we will have to cope with. It is, however, mainly an adult problem.

As I went through the gates yesterday morning I heard a child's voice. The child was calling to me from within his adult prison cell. I looked up at the cold, dirty, concrete wall and examined the windows. There are 28 small, thick, opaque panes of glass set in iron frames in each window, which is recessed into the wall. Built flush against the wall, over each recess, are iron bars also forming 28 squares. Over the iron bars is stretched wire mesh.

Through one, small, opened square a child's hand reached out. The fingers did not, of course, reach the wire mesh. Because the child was small and had to reach upwards

77

from the floor of the cell within, his hand was stretched towards the sky. I could not see his face. I heard only his voice. We have a passing acquaintance from meeting sometimes in the street, this child and I.

He asked me how I was doing. I asked him how he was doing. He said he hadn't seen me around for a while. I remarked that I hadn't seen him around for a while. Lorries were rumbling by and I couldn't hear him very well. He supposed I was going into court. He asked me if I'd be in the Children's Court to see him when he appeared there. Then he got tired and he withdrew his hand and was swallowed up into the darkness behind the small opening.

Jesus only knows how that child passed the day in the Bridewell prison. Or how he had passed the night before. He is there in the company of seven other children. They are, all eight of them, children from the ages of 10 to 14, locked up in prison cells in a holding prison in the centre of Dublin. How would you feel if your small child was in a prison cell? Do you know that it's cold and dark and cheerless there? That there is little difference between day and night, except that during the day you can shout to passers-by? Do you know how silent a cell can be in the middle of the night, and you a child of 10? Do you know that sometimes noises can be heard in the small hours, of shouting, drunken, violent people, who scream and sob, because they do not want to spend even the dawn watch in the Bridewell, as they await trial?

These eight children are itinerants. I do not know if that influenced our cruel, indifferent treatment of them.

They are being held in an adult prison cell because this country, which prosecutes as criminals children from the age of seven upwards, has nowhere else to put them. Institutions which nominally cater for the care of such juvenile offenders refused point blank to take them in. The State, which prosecutes its children, has steadfastly failed to provide a place of shelter for them.

It is quite acceptable for the State to put 10-year-olds in an adult prison. Acceptable, because the State knows that there would not be clamouring thousands gathered outside the Bridewell demanding the release from incarceration of children who should be snuggled into warm beds holding teddy bears.

The massive acquiescent silence is not dependent solely on the fact that these children are itinerants. Other children, from poor areas, have been locked up carelessly in the Bridewell. Mind you, I've never heard of a child from Foxrock being locked up there.

But I musn't be hysterical. Let's not shout. Let's keep calm and quiet. Shush now; go to sleep and forget about it.

24 January 1975

New shoes

The boy-child stood before District Justice Kennedy in the Dublin Children's Court. He was, in a word, dirty. His face was smeared and grimy, his hands filthy, his fingernails totally black. His clothes were covered in dust. Just as one began to wonder why his mother, who sat on the public bench, had not cleaned him for his court appearance, the guard mentioned casually that he had been in police custody since the day before. He wanted a remand, and the boy was released on his mother's bail.

As the boy and his mother left the court to sign the bond, the Justice spoke to the guard. "Has he been sleeping out? He's in an awful condition."

"He's been sleeping out on the buses," said the guard.

"It's dreadful," said the Justice.

The guard told me later that the boy had been held in custody in Fitzgibbon Street station, "on his own request." Whatever the technicalities of holding a child overnight in a police station, and allowing the child to decide where he wants to stay, one question poses itself. Is there no soap and water in a police station? Are there no clothes-brushes? If the guards accept custodial responsibility for a child, should that responsibility not entail elementary practices of hygiene?

After 24 hours in police custody the child appeared in court in what the Justice described as "an awful condition."

Another child pleaded guilty to stealing a pair of shoes from a store. He went in, put on a new pair of shoes, and walked out in them, leaving the old ones behind. He had no previous convictions.

The Justice called the mother of this 12-year-old. "What's this little fellow doing in a city centre store on his own?" she asked the mother.

"I don't know," said the woman.

"You don't know? But you're his mother," said the incredulous Justice.

"Well, I've 11 children, though some of them are married," the mother defended herself.

The Justice turned to the child. "Why did you do it? Tell me why you did it."

The child did not reply.

"You hardly wanted a new pair of shoes," said the Justice.

"No," said the child.

"So you did it for no reason," concluded the Justice. She turned to the mother for confirmation. "Can you explain why he did it? He doesn't want new shoes, does he?"

"Well, he probably could do with a pair," said the mother wistfully.

"Is he a good scholar at school?" asked the Justice.

"He's fair," said the woman, honestly.

"Fair? Is that all?" the Justice reproved. "I'll apply the Probation of Offenders Act. Now, I don't want to see you here ever again. You'll never do that again, will you? Right you be." The boy and his mother left the court. The boy was wearing a pair of busted tennis-shoes.

20 October 1974

God save us and bless us

They didn't come to plead. They came to hustle, and they knew exactly what they wanted. The door of the Children's Court opened and they trotted in, making a busy beeline straight for the Justice's bench. They leaned confidentially over the wooden top, three heads as one, and started chattering to her.

An overnight stay in custody in a Garda station had not improved their appearance. Those three little faces had not seen water in days. Jimmy, in the middle, and the smallest, was the star. His small bum, clad brightly in blue and white striped underpants, protruded unabashed through a gaping split in his wine-coloured trousers. The ladies' shoes, outsize, which he wore, clattered cheerily as he tried to move his feet. His hair was an old-fashioned crew-cut, but thick. "Me mother's sick," he gazed up at the Justice. "In fact," said the guard, "he has left his mother, since the father left, and he stays with this other boy. His parents wouldn't come to court, either."

"Now boys," said the bemused Justice, "did you break and enter such and such a house?" "Yes," chorused her class of three. "And did you break and enter such and such another house?" "yes," they said delightedly.

"And did you break and enter this other house?" "No, no, that was only me," claimed the third boy.

"We'd like to go to St. Laurence's for three months, to keep us out of trouble," said Jimmy, hoisting himself up onto the bench with his elbow, leaving his shoes behind.

"Wait a minute," said the Justice. "Did you enter this other house?" "Yes," they said, "and we'd like to go to St. Laurence's."

"Aren't you the terrible little divils? Aren't you now?" asked the Justice, smiling, as she abandoned all pretence at legal mien. They grinned.

Finally, they had broken into the Jesuit college and stolen cash from the phone booth and mission box, and had been caught in the act.

The parents of Jimmy's friend would not come to court, the guard said, because, they said, the guards were with them every week about the boy, and they wanted him sent to St. Laurence's.

"Yes, St. Laurence's, for three months," they squealed excitedly.

"Why three months?" asked the Justice.

"We'd like to be out for Christmas," explained Jimmy.

"I don't think St. Laurence's will be very glad to receive the three of you," said the Justice. "I'll send you up there until this day week, till we see what we're going to do with you."

"Thanks, thanks," they squealed, and they ran back to the door, nudging each other gleefully. "We're going, we're going," Jimmy joyfully announced to the people outside.

"God save us and bless us," said the Justice to the registrar.

23 October 1974

The Great Van Robbery

In reply to the charge, at the station, the youth had said, "I only said a few words," the guard told District Justice McCarthy in Dublin Children's Court. Before the court stood a boy of cherubic appearance.

"And I think you told him, guard, that the charge was in effect very trivial?", the defence barrister cross-questioned. The guard agreed. "And you had discussions with the alleged injured party, telling him that there was nothing to charge this boy with?", continued the barrister. "In other words, the alleged injured party put pressure on you, demanded that you charge the boy?" The guard agreed.

"He's never been in trouble before?", asked the barrister. The guard agreed. "If it had been up to you, guard, would you have dealt with him by a different procedure?", asked the barrister.

"It's not up to the guard," intervened the Justice.

The Post Office van driver was called to the witness stand.

"I collect mail from boxes in that particular area," he said. "After I had finished one box, and got into my van to drive away, I saw about five or seven youths, I'm not sure of the number, walking down the road. As I was about to move off, I was confronted by this particular youth, who said to me, 'This is a hold-up.' I told him to go away, and I moved off. There was heavy traffic, and I didn't see what happened to him then."

He had met some guards further down then, told them his story, and drove back to where the youths had been. As he pulled in, they ran away, and he gave chase to this particular youth, caught him, and brought both him and the guards back to the station in his van.

"The situation we have here at the moment, I wasn't taking any chances," the man said. "It was dark in this area, and I couldn't see if the youth had anything in his hand when he first approached me."

He and the barrister engaged in argument as to whether it could be so dark in early October, at eight p.m., in a built-up area.

"But in fact you told him to fuck off and he did?", asked the barrister. "That's the expression I used, but I was trying to be polite in court," admitted the man.

"But you were never under the impression that he was going to do anything to you? It was a silly joke and you knew it?", asked the barrister.

"In view of the times we have now, it was no joke," said the man.

"But this is just a boy of 14. He doesn't look any older than that. And he had nothing in his hand and he wasn't going to do anything to you?", continued the barrister.

"Look, it was dark and I couldn't see. I'm not telling any lies," said the man.

"But was it not sufficient punishment to bring the boy to a police station, instead of bringing him to court today, and out of school? Was it not better to have him told off by the guards, rather than have him brought to a criminal court?", asked the barrister.

He had received instructions from the Post Office to go ahead and have the boy charged, said the man. In view of the circumstances when the boy had first approached him, he had been a bit "excited" by the thought of a hold-up.

The barrister asked the Justice to use his discretion in disposing of the matter, because there had been no evidence of any criminal offence.

Section 67 of the Post Office Act, 1908, alleging obstruction of a Post Office official in the due execution of his duty, had been rarely used in court. "This was a joke, played by a boy, on a man in a van," said the barrister.

"This boy intends to join the Army eventually, and these things could be held against him later on, even if there is a conviction without any penalty," he finished.

"I can understand the Post Office man's fear, but it was just a childish prank. I'll dismiss the charge," said the Justice.

Thus ended the saga of the Great Post Office Van Hold-Up, starring one child, one Post Office worker, one guard, one defence barrister and one Justice of the Courts.

17 October 1974

I only hurt myself

Paddy came bouncing into the Dublin Children's court one November morning, in the custody of a guard with whom he was on first name terms. They had just flown in from England, where the guard had gone to collect him and bring him back. Paddy's younger brother had come to court to see him. His mother, who was working in hospital as a cleaner, could not get off work at the short notice given her.

Paddy sat on a bench in the fireplace, his wide smile showing the absence of three front teeth. He proudly adjusted his dangling gold ear-rings and called across to the guard that he was going to miss best English bitter. A naked female was tattooed on his bare right arm. His left arm was buttoned up in a shirt sleeve. His finger joints were also tattooed with letters. His nails were bitten.

He wore a snazzy brown shirt, and a silver buckle belt over brown cords and brown boots. His hair was smartly crew-cut. Paddy liked his own appearance.

The Justice came in and sat down. The guard gave evidence, briefly.

"All three others in this case have been dealt with. I hadn't got time to search through the files but there are a number of charges against the defendant. The facts are, Justice — ".

"Wait", said the Justice. She asked Paddy if he agreed

to be tried by this court. He agreed. She asked him if he had been told of his right to apply for Free Legal Aid.

"I was only brought back from England this morning", said Paddy.

The Justice remanded him in custody for a week, to give him time to see a lawyer.

One week later Paddy reappeared in court, much less bouncily. He smiled warmly at his mother who sat with his seven-year-old sister. Paddy's lawyer who had consulted with him only that morning because she had not heard of the case in time, spoke with the Justice.

"My client has already pleaded guilty to all the charges. He did not turn up for sentencing in September of this year when he was fined £53. He went over to England to look for a job. He had a drug problem before, and was under the care of a doctor. He had been deported from England but now hopes for a job here, delivering coal and turf."

She paused.

"My client has just spent a week in custody in St. Patrick's. Last Sunday he slashed his left arm there. He did this once before, in custody, Justice. He seems to have a self-destructive impulse. If he is sentenced, this may occur again. He has seen the psychiatrist in St. Patrick's . . . if he is released, he will try for a place in Coolmine, which helps drug offenders. There is a strict regime there and they are not allowed out. They are not entitled to work there. If there is any money due them from social welfare, it is taken off them to cover the cost of being there . . .

"There are 12 children in the family. The father left them some years ago . . . since the last offence my client has not instigated any further action to get money from drugs, Justice."

"I'll put the case back for six months to see how he gets on", said the Justice. And that was that.

Paddy walked out, free now and without court supervision, with his mother and baby sister. Whether or not he goes for treatment is up to himself, assuming that Coolmine will accept him. It is a voluntary institution.

Two mornings later I went to visit them in a pleasant housing estate. The home was neat and cheerful, lacking only carpet on the bare stairs. Paddy lay on the carpet in front of the livingroom fire, his head sleepily on his mother's knees. He had not been to bed since leaving the Castle, his mother said, because there were outstanding charges against him, from a long time since, and he was keeping vigil lest the guards call round. He planned to run out the back.

"Paddy doesn't like being locked up," the woman said. Her son reminded her of the time he had a burst abscess — she thought it was food poisoning — in St. Patrick's, and he was rushed to hospital. There were complications after the operation and he remained in hospital for five months, with tubes up his nose and back passage.

"When I got out they brought me back to St. Pat's to finish the last week of my sentence."

He had spent three out of the last four Christmases in jail. "Maybe I'll see this Christmas at home," he grinned.

I asked him if he was not going to the drug clinic. He thought he might go in January, if the police hadn't picked him up again or he wasn't in England. He had liked being over there, getting £30 a week on social welfare.

"I wish he could get off the drugs," his mother said. She asked Patrick to show me his slashes. There was a wide, raised gash, old and covered with pale skin tissue, running from his wrist up to his left forearm. Parallel to it was a new thin pink one that he had inflicted on himself with a razor in St. Patrick's a few days hence.

"They're supposed to check the razors for blades after shaving but they didn't bother last Sunday." A thin gash encircled his throat. "I did that on the roof in Summerhill, I'd just been on cocaine and booze. I don't know why I do it," he said jauntily.

The mother said she had moved from Summerhill in an effort to get Paddy away from trouble. She had done this long before the Corpo had decided to close Summerhill. She and Paddy recalled his early years. He drank, took drugs, stole cars, snatched handbags, saw probation officers, tried to kill himself regularly.

Only one other of the 12 children was in trouble with the law. The woman brought out of her handbag his 17 charge sheets, saying there were more upstairs.

"You'd need a computer to figure them out. It says on this one, he stole in Raheny at two in the morning, then at Ballsbridge at five. How could he cross the city in that time, in the middle of the night? Still, he did some of these things, I know that, but the police clear their books with him any time they catch him."

The guards, she said, call regularly at her home, any time there's been a break-in.

"The ones from Raheny have manners on them. But the Coolock guards — they come at dawn. He always signs a confession. He's even signed for things Paddy hasn't done."

She tried always to turn up in court for the two sons, though she had sometimes to bring the younger children along and it was expensive to travel.

When the sons were being charged at the police station she had to go along to witness, but she might be there for hours while they were being interrogated.

"I had to give up the job at the hospital. The children like me to be at home when they come in from school."

Her eldest son, aged 20, had a trade and did not approve of Paddy, "so there's friction. I mean, I can't take his wages and give money out of it to Paddy. I do be torn." Another son had taken a flat on his own. Another son stayed with an aunt.

She went out to the kitchen to make tea and called Paddy after her. I heard her ask him to borrow butter from next door. She brought the tea in with one buttered sugar-bun each.

Paddy showed me the upstairs bedroom he shared with a brother. There were posters on the walls and a specially erected spotlight on "Elvis the King." He was "crushed" when he heard in St. Patrick's that the King was dead. He played for me the record on Pope John Paul that the others had bought for his mother. He showed me the pigeons his younger brother kept in the backyard.

We went back downstairs and returned to the story. They talked of police and courts and charges as intimately and continuously as other people talk of relatives. They hoped that the recently jailed social worker, whom they knew — "he's very nice" — would speak out about jail conditions.

"The younger boy now, that has all these charges, he spent 18 months in Lusk industrial school, but then he walked out, and didn't finish his time. No, they don't come to pick him up again. They are not obliged to keep anyone there. You saw yourself last week how he was able to go to court to see Paddy."

Paddy speculated about his chances of buying a horse and cart. "There's a killing to be made now with this coal strike." That was the prospective job his lawyer had referred to in court. Paddy had once worked with a horse and cart, when he was 11.

"Or maybe I'll hit the drugs again and slash meself. One of these days I'll be a goner." His mother winced. He hugged her legs. "At least, now, I'm not like me da. I don't hurt you. I only hurt myself."

She wondered how much it had cost for the guard to fly over and back from England, bringing Paddy with him. "And all for to turn him out onto the street again. He never slashed himself in England. I don't think he'll ever see Coolmine."

Paddy was asleep on the floor.

1–2 January 1980

The care of children

Because their case was next to be heard, the parties were asked to leave the draughty waiting room of Dublin's Children's Court and go upstairs, where they milled on the narrow landing outside the court-room. There was not much space. The social worker with the baby in his arms was allowed to step into the warm administrative office that adjoined the landing.

The others stood outside, getting in each other's way. Fifteen people in a confined space. There was only one chair, seven of them were smoking. Their ashes and butts and matches littered the floor. The children stood in this dirt, in a haze of tobacco smoke.

Their case was called and they went in, taking their seats on the benches before Justice Eileen Kennedy. The elderly woman, wrinkled and spare, kept her arm around a boy. The young woman took a girl. One of the men, eyes puffed like a boxer, took a two-year-old boy in his arms. The social worker sat behind them with the girl baby.

A lawyer for the Eastern Health Board outlined the situation.

A total of four children were involved. Mary and Paddy were the married parents of two of them. The marriage broke up, and Paddy, who kept the two children, set up home with Patricia who already had one child. Patricia and Paddy then had a fourth child between them.

That relationship, too, broke up.

Mary and Paddy were now in court, with a lawyer who represented their two legal children, but Patricia had not come, though the case had been adjourned several times to facilitate her and she knew this was the final hearing. Patricia's mother, however, granny to two of the children, was present.

A doctor was called who testified that the youngest baby had been brought to hospital by Paddy, suffering from an eye infection. He described the baby as poorly looked after, dirty and with poor weight. When the baby was not brought back for a further examination, as requested, a District Nurse visited the home three times, receiving no reply at any time.

The baby was admitted to hospital for treatment some months later. The doctor agreed in court that Paddy had brought the baby in the second time, and that the child was released back into the custody of Paddy and Patricia one week later, though a social worker had been alerted.

A social worker then testified that she had first contacted the family in June, 1977, at the time of Paddy's marriage to Mary, when they were staying in army married quarters in Cathal Brugha barracks.

She described the army accommodation as "very poor". By June 1978, the marriage with Mary was broken and Paddy now lived with Patricia, and things were going very well. They were rearing three children.

In December 1978 they moved to army married quarters in Griffith Barracks. The social workers thought conditions here very poor indeed, with broken windows, a cold water tap, no bathroom and no toilet. Patricia had given birth to a baby without receiving any ante-natal care.

The social worker made several efforts to have her receive post natal care, driving her to and from the clinic. On a couple of occasions she called at the flat while it was snowing, to find windows broken and no fires lighting. Patricia was not well after the birth and had to spend some mornings in bed, but some mornings she found both Patricia and Paddy asleep in bed, with the children unattended in the back bedroom.

Neither of the two school-age children was attending school.

The accommodation provided by the army consisted of one poorly furnished livingroom, a kitchen and two bedrooms. She never noticed marks of physical abuse but the two-year-old child, Mary's son, seemed very withdrawn and frightened, cowering away from people, though the social worker saw him several times a week.

A guard testified that as the result of a call earlier this year he went to Griffith Barracks one morning and found an untidy house, with a wet livingroom floor and a young baby lying naked there in a pram. The baby appeared to be hungry. There were three other children in a back bedroom. There were no adults there. He called an ambulance and had the children removed to hospital.

A second social worker testified that Patricia and Paddy had broken up, come together again, and broken up finally this year. The four children were now in care.

The solicitor engaged to represent the two legal children said that Paddy's brother and sister-in-law hoped to become foster parents to them and had come to court. The Eastern Health Board solicitor interrupted to say that

90

Patricia, mother of the other two children, had now arrived in court. Patricia took her baby from the arms of the social worker and sat behind her mother, who held Patricia's other child.

Paddy was called to the stand. He said that on the morning the guard called he had gone out to work as a member of the army. He had had an argument the night previously with Patricia, did not realise she had then walked out, and thought that she was in the back bedroom with the eldest children, though he did not check. He waited until 9.30 in the livingroom that morning though he was supposed to start work at 8.30.

He had got his eldest daughter, by Mary, into school for one day. He could not get Patricia's son into school because Patricia hadn't got the birth certificate. He wanted his brother and the brother's wife to look after his two legal children now, and he would contribute money to their upkeep.

The brother, who earned good money in the transport business, testified that he had a three bedroomed home with a garden. He had often baby-sat the children, and he wanted to foster two of them now. His wife testified that they would love to foster since they had no children of their own. She would give up her job as secretary to do so.

The Justice asked if Mary, Paddy's legal wife, wanted to tell the court anything. Mary stood up from her bench, said "No," and sat down again between the brother and his wife.

The Justice asked if Patricia had anything to say. Patricia went to the front of the court and sat on the chair. The Justice asked her if she would object to an order committing her own two children into care.

"You can take care of them till I get a place of my own," said Patricia. She was short and dark, with running mascara.

A social worker said that the brother and wife would have to be vetted as prospective foster parents before consideration could be given to their fostering anybody. The process of vetting should take three months.

The Justice committed all four children into care, the baby to be separated to Madonna House, which looks after infants.

The case closed, and all parties filed out and downstairs. The waiting room was too dirty and public and cold so they moved outside into the November sunshine that wanly warmed the vast empty square. Patricia stood with the baby in her arms, alongside her mother, and the baby's guardian. The two eldest children played with a social worker, nearby. A fourth child received hugs and caresses from the brother and his wife. While Mary, its legal mother, stood alongside them, her neck in a brace.

Two other social workers stood with the lawyers, discussing things. Paddy wandered among the groupings, touching children on the head. The social workers and the lawyers answered questions from the two mothers, the granny, the father, the prospective foster parents, as the children shifted about, enjoying the attention being showered on them from all sides.

It took them half an hour to sort matters out, standing and moving in the open air. Nobody dreamt of going back into the filthy building. Finally the children were dispersed into two cars. Paddy ran after one car, waving as it sped down the street. His wife walked along with the brother and his wife. Patricia and her mother moved along some distance behind them, three separate groupings with nothing in common but the departing children.

I went to Griffith Barracks. Bobby Molloy, then Minister for Defence, had made a Senate speech some days previously about the induction of women into the army. Women would be allowed to resign on marriage or pregnancy, if they wished, because of the "recognition of the importance which our society attaches to family life and the care of children."

Griffith Barracks, where army families are housed, is a dump. It is literally a dump. The unpaved open ground, around which three two-storey buildings form a triangle, is littered with bedsprings, parts of cars, rubbish and the remains of a large bonfire. They melt well with the natural dirt of the ground.

An open catwalk, protected by metal railings, gives onto the flats on the upper storey. At either end of the catwalk are the communal toilets which families must use, walking along its exposed length in rain, wind, snow, sleet and darkness, even in the middle of the night. Most of the toilets are filthy, some are broken, all of them are of bare brick.

They are dark smelly places. None of the flats has bathrooms. One woman I spoke with was raising three daughters in a one-bedroom unit. Pressure of space means they keep coal in boxes outside their front doors and string their washing from the catwalks or on the waste ground around the barracks.

Such is the importance which the Irish Army under Bobby Molloy attaches to family life. Children who were taken from these barracks in need of care subsequently appeared in the Children's Court, another dirty, cold and miserable building with stinking toilets. Social workers could not bear to see children in either of these State-run institutions. They preferred instead to gather, with children, in the vast open courtyard of Dublin Castle. A wide-open stony square is the best accommodation this State had to offer the children of this nation.

3 January 1980

Chapter 7
Regulars

"My client is 21 years old and is a qualified mechanic," the solicitor told District Justice Ó hUadhaigh in Dublin District Court 6.

"Is he?" the justice commented.

"At the time of the offences, he was unemployed," said the solicitor.

"I must point out to you," the justice cut in, "that at the time of the offences, there was a warrant out for his arrest, because he failed to turn up to answer another charge. I'm just pointing that out. While you're talking, you can be thinking about it."

"My client was reared in an orphanage," the solicitor resumed, "and the most unfortunate thing about that is, that when he got older, there was nowhere to keep him except Daingean Reformatory, though he had never been convicted of any crime, and there he had to associate with boys who had been convicted of crime."

"All this talk, you know," interrupted the justice, "is very nice, but many a lad was sent to public school in England, and learnt things there that he shouldn't have learnt, from other boys, and his parents paying astronomical fees to keep him there.

"That's life. That's life," the justice concluded philosophically.

Among English public schools, Harrow and Shrewsbury are highly regarded. Harrow produced Winston Churchill. Shrewsbury produced Charles Darwin, who wrote *The*

Origin of Species. There are perhaps, some Irish people who think that Winston Churchill was a bad lot, and probably even more Irish people who think that Charles Darwin was a bad influence.

In the dock of the Dublin District Court sat Paddy Murphy. alumnus of Daingean Reformatory. The 1970 Government report on Industrial and Reform schools in the Republic of Ireland recommended that Daingean "be closed at the earliest possible moment." When the school was inspected, the report said, "the boys were illdressed and dirty and there was a general air of neglect about the place . . . the kitchen and refectory are situated in what were formerly the stables and are depressing and decayed . . . the toilets were dirty and insanitary . . . the showers were corroded through lack of use, and the hot water system was so inadequate that the boys seldom if ever washed in hot water.

"The committee members were so perturbed about conditions that they sent a request to the Minister for Education asking that immediate specific steps be taken to ameliorate conditions there."

The solicitor listened to the justice's equation of Daingean Reformatory with English public schools and murmured: "I would ask you to keep in mind, justice, that his background was not an entirely happy one."

"I always have sympathy for orphans," the justice responded. "The court must have due consideration for children who have been deprived of association with parents. That association is absolutely essential, there's no doubt about that, if they're good parents."

"In addition," said the solicitor, "my client's mother, who is in court today, married later on, and my client didn't get on with his stepfather."

"That happens. That happens," said the justice sagely.

"So that situation didn't help him either," said the solicitor. "In relation to these charges, my client wishes to make restitution for the unrecovered property."

Paddy Murphy, the solicitor continued, had a job offer from the garage where he had learned his trade.

"Anything else?" the justice asked.

"No. That's all I have to say." The solicitor sat down.

"Don't stop now just because I — , " began the justice. "I mean to say, do you want to call his mother, for instance?" "No," said the solicitor.

"I think you're well advised not to," said the justice. He pondered the case before him. Paddy Murphy had 20 previous convictions, the last three recorded in December, 1974, and January, 1975, when he had been sentenced to prison, for 12 months in all, for larceny offences.

He had currently pleaded guilty to about 20 more offences, committed in November and December of 1975, shortly after release from prison. He had stolen, from cars and private dwellings, property amounting to £600 in value, of which only £100 worth had been recovered. He also pleaded guilty to taking away a car without the owner's consent and driving without insurance.

The justice was concerned about the fact that these latest offences had been committed while Paddy Murphy was out on bail on other charges, and that Paddy Murphy had not answered his bail. The police had been looking for him, with a warrant for his arrest. "The terrible thing is", said the justice, "that you were released in station bail. Warrants were out for your arrest, and a station sergeant set you free to go out and commit more offences . . . the responsibility for that rests on the sergeant who released you and on nobody else. It's inconceivable to the court that somebody could be released on station bail while a warrant was out for him."

The defendant, said the justice, "had clearly no regard for other people's property, or for law and order or for the courts".

The defendant had so far committed one offence for every year of his life. Or rather, the justice revised his arithmetic, he had started crime at 16, was now 20, or was it 21, and had therefore committed four, or was it five, offences every year. And in fact, the justice revised again, if one took into account the 20 current charges, that worked out at . . .

The justice dropped the mathematics and went into the defendant's background. "While I will take regard of the plea of guilty, and will take into consideration the lack of home life as a small child, I must also put into the balance what you have done and it completely outweighs these other matters. I can't see how, in justice to the community, I can give you less than the maximum sentence".

Indeed, the justice continued, it was "unfortunate" that the Director of Public Prosecutions had decided to have the offences dealt with in the lower courts, because in his view, the defendant merited "more severe treatment than that which is about to be meted out".

A "trivial £100 worth of property had been recovered out of £600 worth", the justice warmed to a finale, and he was now imposing "a sentence of 12 months imprisonment, and driving licence to be suspended for ten years" for driving without insurance.

He fixed bail for appeal at an independent surety of £500, justifying the enormous amount by Paddy Murphy's failure to appear in court on other occasions.

Paddy Murphy, garage mechanic, with a ten-year suspended licence, convicted thief, alumnus of the country's orphanages and reformatories, went off to prison.

Daingean Reformatory was closed following publication of the Government report in 1970. But Paddy had left it by then.

14 January 1976

Now stay out of trouble

The guard told Distict Justice Good in Dublin District Court 4 that as he had been sitting in his car, at traffic lights, off-duty, and in the company of his wife, two youths had tried to open his door. The lights changed to green and he managed to close the door, and drive off. He identified the youth in the dock as the one who had tried to open his door.

The youth vigorously denied that he had opened, or attempted to open, the car door. His mate might have done it, he allowed, while "messing about", but he himself had just happened to be one of the crowd. He had resisted arrest because he was just out of jail and got excited, especially at the idea of going back to the police station. The girls who were with him that day would tell the justice that he had not opened the car door.

The justice asked him if he had any witnesses. The youth looked back to the public benches. But the two girls who had come to court with him had been put out by the court guard because they had laughed once, at something that had been said during the case. The youth said he had no witness. The justice convicted.

The youth had five previous convictions, the guard said. He had received a two months' suspended sentence in May, 1973, for larceny. In July, 1973, the Juvenile Court had committed him to St. Patrick's Institution for one month for assault. In September, 1973, he had received a 12-month sentence, reduced to six on appeal, for breaking and entering and larceny. In February last he had got 12 months for robbery with violence.

"He had just been out two weeks when this happened," the guard said, "and other charges have been heard against him. He was up for a breach of the peace since."

"There was no robbery with violence," the youth said. "I was just robbing offices."

"You served most of the 12 months given you in February," commented the justice.

"No, I served nearly every bit of it," said the youth.

"You got no remission?" asked the justice.

"I lost my remission," said the youth angrily.

"That's not good. That means you weren't a good prisoner," said the justice. "You weren't behaving yourself."

"Is there any chance I could get a chance now?" asked the youth. He was not pleading. It was simply that he had nothing to lose by asking. "I've been in trouble since I was born. I've always been in prison of one kind or another. I was raised in Letterfrack and Daingean and St. Patrick's and Mountjoy. I'm always in trouble. I can't help it."

"Have you ever tried to help yourself?" asked the justice. "If you can't help yourself somebody had better restrain you."

"Look. I've spent the last four Christmases in jail," said the youth. "I want to go straight, but I never get a chance."

"If you got out today, where would you go?" asked the justice.

"I got a visit during the week from me aunt and she said if I got off I could go to her, and she'd get me a job and all."

"You're very wild," said the justice.

"I want to be free at Christmas," said the youth, frantically.

"Don't worry about Christmas. Worry about your future. Christmas is only a side issue," said the justice. "If the case were remanded for a few months, perhaps you could pull yourself together."

He decided to remand the case until February to see if the youth's aunt could get him a job. "But if I get a bad report then from the guards, I'll send you back to jail, though I don't want to. Prison doesn't seem to have a reforming effect on you, nor is it a deterrent to you. Now stay out of trouble."

The question of bail came up. The youth had been in custody for a week, because no one could be found to go bail for him. The justice released him in his own bail of £25. The youth went off to the bails office.

I went out to the court corridor. Students who had just been bailed out, and their friends, were excitedly talking. There were about 15 of them in all.

I went over to speak to the youth who had spent his life in prison. He had been sent away to institutions as a child, he told me, because his parents weren't fit to look after him.

He didn't like Artane, and he escaped and was recaptured and sent to Daingean. "From then on, it was just trouble. Me parents died in 1971. Or was it 1970? It doesn't matter . . ."

Just then the guard came out who had earlier put the youth's two girl-friends out of the court. "You," he said to the youth, "get out of here."

"I'm talking to him," I said.

"Get you out too," he said. "No talking in the corridor."

"The students over there are talking," I said, pointing
to the mass of students, still chattering away.

"Get out of here," the guard said pushing the youth
down the stairs.

The youth moved off. I asked him to come back and
talk to me. The guard pushed me.

"Ah, you can't fucking win. If I don't go, they'll do me
again," said the youth and he went away.

The students continued talking, all fifteen of them.

The guard went back into the courtroom.

And that's how the law operates.

4 December 1974

The quiet man

The man in the dock was neatly, competently dressed,
much in the manner of single middle-aged men, who move
greyly about, and quietly, attracting no attention at all.
He stood in the dock of Dublin District Court 6, before
District Justice Ua Donnchadha, and pleaded guilty to
breaking and entering a camera shop on the night of
January 13th.

He broke the window of the shop and removed some
cameras. When arrested, he admitted the offence freely.
He said he had sold the cameras in pubs for £14, said the
prosecuting guard. He had convictions dating back to
1951. The last three were all in 1973, said the guard:
two six months' sentences for breaking and entering,
malicious damage and larceny and a 12 months' sentence
for house-breaking with intent.

"Did you serve that 12 months?" the Justice asked
him.

"I think I did," he said, indifferent as he was to the
mental effort of working out for the Justice exactly
when and how often he had been in jail.

"You think you did?" echoed the Justice, surprised
that a person could not remember such a major event.
But he was talking to a man for whom prison was a second

home.

"If the guard could tell me the date," said the man. "I must have served it though, if it's written down there."

The guard said that the man had been released in February 1974.

"I was released on the fifth of February," said the man, who remembered that major date very clearly.

"Are you married?" asked the Justice.

"I'm single," he replied.

"What age are you?"

"I'm 43."

"Do you have any occupation?"

"None."

"How do you exist?"

"I get the labour, £6.35 a week."

"In other words you are unemployed," said the Justice.

"He worked until January," said the guard, "and then he lived in the Salvation Army hostel."

"Is there anything you want to say about this offence?" asked the Justice.

"There's nothing I can say, your honour," said the man. You could feel that he saw the writing on the wall.

"Well, you just can't do this. That's all," said the Justice, uselessly. "That's what the law says. You can't do this. Very well. I have no option but to commit you to prison. The cameras were worth £193 and that's all there is to it. I'm sentencing you to nine months' imprisonment."

The man, much in the manner of recidivists for whom we provide no option, moved quietly and greyly out of the dock, and down the stairs to the cell and eventual imprisonment, attracting no attention at all.

25 January 1975

The kind of man I admire

The youth, who had previously pleaded guilty to numerous charges of housebreaking and larceny, had been remanded for a medical report. In Dublin District Court No. 4 District Justice Good told the defence solicitor that the medical report and the welfare report both recommended

St. Patrick's.

The guard, referring to one sheet, said that the amount should be reduced from £70 to £4, which the guard would accept was all that the youth had got from the proceeds. His companions had been charged already.

"From the reports," said the defence solicitor, "it does appear that my client's behaviour indicates personality problems. He is immature, of a dull intellect, and his family environment is not desirable. The father is a good man, but he was away most of the time, and the mother was unable to cope with 16 children. The father is 40 years of age and is an impressively young man, despite the fact of having a large family. He has done overseas service with the Army, but retired this year, earlier than, in fact, he need have, because of these family problems. He retired in order to provide the leadership, stability and control which was lacking. It is not always easy for a man to choose the profession he wants, and his choice of profession involved a large absence from home.

"The report says this boy is easily led and not inclined to undertake any activity, important or unimportant, without a companion. I note that a large amount of property was taken, of which little was recovered. My client has had some of it stolen from him. His actions arose more from mischief and circumstances than from greed.

"He is not very good at looking after himself, nor is he acquisitive. He has tried to get a job, but he became disheartened, as the report points out. I've been speaking with the guard in the case and it seems to be a situation where it would be worthwhile to have some sort of social service for him. He's still young enough to learn."

The Justice remarked that the youth had already done three months in St. Patrick's, in 1972, for the unauthorised taking away of a motor-car, and had received a three-month suspended sentence in the same year for housebreaking.

The guard said that the youth always acted with others who were more intelligent than himself. Two boys had committed a crime in the area last week and had bought tickets to England from the proceeds. They had hoped to take this youth with them, but he wouldn't go. He had failed to appear in court on a former occasion, more through fear of the court than anything else. He needed help of some kind, the guard finished.

The Justice said that the youth must bear some burden of the responsibility and that the situation presented a problem as to what to do. He asked if anyone had any suggestions. The solicitor said that the father, in conjunction with a social worker, might be able to help. "I think you'll be impressed by the father. He's going to be around more than he was in the past," finished the solicitor.

The father took the stand. He was indeed an impressively young-looking man.

"How many children still remain at home?" asked the solicitor. The father thought a moment, and the solicitor said: "Put it this way. How many have left home?"

"One," the father replied. He had 15 children at home, ranging in age from 20 years to six months.

"That is a heavy responsibility," commented the Justice.

"That's why I left the Army, where I had been for 20 years," said the father.

"Is your wife able to cope?" asked the Justice.

"Well, she sent me a letter saying they were getting out of hand," said the father.

"It's a very big responsibility and I don't envy you," said the Justice. "I don't mean I don't envy you having a big family. People like having a lot of children, but it's a heavy responsibility for the father."

(It's a heavy responsibility for the mother too.)

"Maybe with me at home all the time I'll be able to curtail his activities," said the father.

The Justice said that the area they lived in was not too good. "The boy is not very bright," continued the Justice. "Without labouring the matter, I think with men like the Probation Officer and yourself, and notwithstanding all the charges, I'd be prepared to take a gamble, particularly now that you're at home and able to exercise a paternal influence.

"You're the kind of man I admire. You've given service to your country and brought a big family into the world.

You're a man I'd have great trust in."

The Justice asked the 18-year-old youth if he'd do what his father told him and if he appreciated the eloquence of his solicitor. The youth nodded his head. The Justice remanded the case until next March, when, he requested the father and son, they should appear to give a progress report.

4 December 1973

Beggared

"Are you guilty or not guilty," District Justice Ó hUadhaigh asked the old man in Dublin District Court 6. "Well, I don't remember anything," replied the defendant. "That's not guilty then. Anyway you're not charged with being drunk — it's wandering abroad and begging," the district justice said.

He was sitting in the St. Stephen's Green area, the cap held out in his hand, asking people for money, the garda said. "Had I any money in my cap?" the man asked him. "No, no money," the garda said, "but people had to walk around to get past you."

"I'd just took bad," the man muttered. "Was he looking sick?" the district justice asked the garda. "I heard him saying something about taking bad . . ." "No," replied the garda, "he just said to me he'd had a few pints."

"I had and all sir," the old man said, "I had a good drink, and I was makin' me way home to Merrion Gates . . ." (Merrion Gates is a voluntary shelter run for the winos).

"There's no harm sitting down, as long as you don't obstruct the public highway," said District Justice Ó hUadhaigh.

"I only had five or six shillings in me pocket," said the man, "and I took bad. I wasn't interfering with anybody. I sat down, and I took off me cap, it's a habit I have when I'm sitting down."

"Convict," decided the district justice.

The man had 12 previous convictions for begging, the garda said. The last was on April 12th, when he had received a one-month sentence, suspended.

"Ah well, he's not getting a suspended this time," said District Justice Ó hUadhaigh briskly. "One month's imprisonment. Away with ye, come on, one month."

The next defendant had been sitting about 30 yards away from the previous defendant, the garda said.

He was pleading guilty. He had received a one-month suspended sentence for a similar offence in July, 1972. "Why'd you do it?" District Justice Ó hUadhaigh asked the man who was charged with begging.

"Well, me mother and father's living out in Dun Laoghaire," explained the man, "though me father's in hospital at the moment. Now, I get drunk. I'll tell you the truth. I got drunk and I done a bit of begging. Me mother and father's a bit too old, I don't like discommodin' them when I'm drunk . . . I'm married with six kids, but me wife's left me and I lost me house in Ballyfermot. . . at the moment I'm unemployed."

"What was your father when he was working?" asked the district justice.

"Oh, he wasn't working," said the man.

"Convict," said the district justice, turning to the garda; "what'd he say to you when you came along? Was he half-drunk?"

"We gave him every opportunity to leave. He had a few shillings in his cap and pockets," replied the garda. "I was trying to make the money for the Iveagh hostel," said the man, "I only get £4.35 on the labour, and it's 10 bob a night there."

"That's all right," the Justice assured him. "One month's imprisonment, warrant not to issue. Were you ever here for anything except begging?"

"I was here for drunk and disorderly, but I done me time," said the man.

"All right. One month, not to issue for six months, on condition that you're of good behaviour during that time. You come back again, you'll go to jail, is that clear to you?"

"Oh, yes, thank you, me honour," said the man gratefully.

18 May 1973

Monotonous regularity

The thin man came up the steps from the cell, and leaned on his crutch in the dock of Dublin District Court 6 before District Justice Ua Donnchadha. The guard took the oath and the man sat down.

"I found the defendant drunk and incapable . . . he was lying on the footpath fast asleep. He seemed to be almost unconscious from drink," the guard said. It happened on Thursday afternoon between two and three p.m.

The man had no questions to ask. "Do you admit that it is true?", asked the justice.

"I had a lot of drink taken," said the man gently.

"How old are you?", asked the justice.

He was 37. His beard gave him youth. His ankle was broken.

"Do you work?", asked the justice.

Sometimes, but not since he had broken his ankle.

"Do you know anything about him?", the justice turned to the guard.

"I have not got his record of previous convictions here," said the guard, "but he turns up in court with monotonous regularity. I think the last time was a fort-night ago."

"Six weeks," said the man softly.

"What were you here for?", asked the justice.

"Drunk," said the man simply.

"And what happened to you? Were you fined?", asked the justice.

"£2", said the man.

"Do you get any money from anyone? Are you in re-ceipt of social security benefits, or anything like that?", asked the justice.

"No", said the man, "I know a few people," he added, with dignity.

He had no fixed abode. The Simon Community looked after him.

"Well, I don't know," said the justice. "I'll apply the Probation Act. This man sins more against himself than anything."

I suppose it would be out of the question for guards to return sinners with monotonous regularity to the community which cares for them?

26 July 1975

Christmas is coming

"I arrested the two defendants between 11 and 12 midnight last night", the guard told District Justice Johnston in Dublin District Court 4. "They were fighting and were drunk on the public highway".

The guard rested his case.

"Do you wish to ask the guard anything?", the Justice inquired. "No", said one of the defendants. "Are you pleading?", asked the Justice. "I'm guilty, yes", said the same defendant.

"Two pounds fine against each defendant, payable forthwith, or seven days' in default", said the Justice.

"Ah, excuse me", said the defendant. "I'm at present working, and I'd be able to give you the money on Friday if you give me a chance".

"You have no fixed abode", said the Justice.

"I have", said the defendant.

"He gave me an address, but I don't think he's stayed there for quite some time now", said the guard. "He tells me he works four days a week for the Redemptorist fathers".

"I won't change my order", said the Justice, and he rose and left the bench.

It was a quarter to twelve and the courtroom was empty.

The two defendants stayed standing in the dock. The guard was in no hurry to take them below. It was that kind of lazy day. One of the defendants was middle-aged. The other was a young boy. Both had cuts on their faces, testifying to their debacle the night before. They stood there, with a week in prison ahead of them because they didn't have £2 each.

Being of no fixed abode, they could not be trusted to pay the fine, eventually, should the Justice have freed them. And if they hadn't paid the fine the guards would have to go round the city looking for them. Or institute a nationwide search or something. A £2 fine is a heavy thing after all. The State would go broke without it.

So, because they couldn't pay all that money they were sent off to prison. Where they will occupy two prison cells for a week. And be watched over by prison officers for a week. Forms will have to be filled in to record their presence there. Administrative details will have to be detailed to account for them.

Because they were drunk on the public highway and fighting. They'll be released on Christmas Eve. And they'll be broke. And they won't have had time like the rest of us to make Christmas arrangements.

But, on the other hand, they're only two bums. Sure they wouldn't have arrangements to make like the rest of us. What's a week out of their lives? Take them off the face of the city and lock them away out of sight. If they'd paid the £2 each we wouldn't have been put to all that expense, would we?

This'll teach them.

19 December 1974

Making a success of life

He had curling hair and a thin beard, and black shoes, and the jacket of a suit that did not match the pants. His clothes and face were stained, and he was skinny and he had left his forties behind him. Before District Justice Ó hUadhaigh in Dublin District Court No. 4 he was charged with wandering abroad and begging.

"I saw the defendant in the street," said the prosecuting guard, "and he was putting out his hand and asking people for money. Some people refused him, and he followed them and obstructed them. I had previously cautioned him. As I was arresting him and putting him into the car a woman came up and told me that he had bothered her and . . ."

"You can't introduce that part," said the Justice. "Has he been here before?" He had been in court on October 2nd for the same offence. "What do you want to say about this?", the Justice asked. The man spoke in a stammering, thick disjointed mumble, and I could not understand him. "Have you anything to say as to why I should not send you to jail?", asked the Justice. "I met a few friends," said the man, "and . . . and . . . and this is the last chance I have, your honour."

"I remember," said the Justice, "I think it was four or five years ago in Court 6, pointing out to you what you were heading for, and you didn't accept the advice I gave you, I told you you were heading for Mountjoy."

The man foot-dragged down the stairs. He had been in jail often before for begging, the guards said later.

In Court No. 6, on the same day, before District Justice Good, a young businessman was convicted of obtaining several hundred pounds by false pretences. He bounced cheques. It was his first offence, and he received a nine-month suspended sentence and left the court a free man. "I think you are a very inexperienced, immature and irresponsible young man," the Justice said. "I think you showed gross recklessness to show the least of it . . . but I have to take into account . . . your previous blameless record and character . . . I'm very sorry to see you in this position . . . I feel that I am treating you with the leniency I think you are entitled to in this case because of your previous good record. You struck me as being very intelligent, and in the process of time you will probably be a great success, and I think you have the capacity to make a success of your life."

2 November 1973

Chapter 8
Three People

Rosie

The old woman was drunk, the garda said. "I was drunk Justice," she said. "How are you now, are you sober?" Justice Ó hUadhaigh asked her and she replied, "Well, partly."

She'd been there from early morning, the garda said, lying on the footpath at St. Stephen's Green. "Sure you'll be dead someday, Rosie," the district justice said, "it's terrible. All right, fined £1. Have you any money?" "I don't know," she said, "You'll have to ask the officer if I did."

"She was getting some money from the public for the pictures she sold," said the garda, "I'm sure she has some." (She had been selling little holy pictures). She shook her head.

"Ah, sure Rosie, you want a rest," said the Justice. "One pound or 14 days imprisonment, if it's not paid immediately."

For an awful moment I thought he was going to say 14 days in the Shelbourne.

26 May 1973

* * *

Before District Justice Kearney, in court 5, an old woman appeared. She carried her belongings in a plastic bag. A lady took the stand and was sworn in. She was employed in a woman's hostel, she said. "I was in the dining-hall and I saw the accused throw a bottle through the window."

"Did she do this deliberately or what?" asked the guard.

"Yes," said the lady," she did it for no reason at all."

"Do you have any questions to ask?" the justice asked the old woman.

"Ah, well, no," she said. Then she changed her mind. "Ah, yes, if I may ask her just one question." She addressed herself to the lady. "How can you say I done it for no reason at all? How can you say that? Could you say anything about what caused me to do it?"

"There was no reason," said the lady.

"No reason that you could see," the justice put it more legally.

"Nobody said anything to her, she had no cause to do it," the lady said.

The damage was estimated at £28, the guard said, producing a sheet of paper.

"Did you get a proper estimate?" asked the justice.

"I got this this morning from the woman in charge of the hostel," said the guard.

"But she's not in court, is she? Have you no other way of proving the damage?" asked the justice. The guard had no other way.

"The proofs don't go far enough," said the justice, dismissing the charge on a technicality. The old woman walked out with her plastic bag.

19 October 1973

* * *

Rosie appeared yet again in the District Court. The prosecuting guard held up the child's coat stolen ineptly, inevitably, from a city store. She was, of course, drunk at the time. She always gets caught. The guard said on her last appearance that she just lifts things, and doesn't really know what she's doing. Her actions vary from time to time. Once she broke a window in the hostel where she stayed.

Now, she told District Justice Good, in Dublin District Court 4, she had £5.18 a week income. Of this she used to pay £2 a week rent to the hostel, but they put her out after she broke a window there. The charge had been dismissed in court (because of failure to prove the amount of damage), but when she had returned that night to the hostel, "they asked me to pay another £2 a week, on top of the rent, to pay for the window. I hadn't got it, and they put me out."

"You were asked to pay £2 towards the window and you didn't pay anything?", asked the Justice.

"Sure they didn't give me time to pay it, sir," said Rosie. "I went in that night and they asked me for £2 and I said I hadn't got it and they told me to go and put me out, by the guards. There's the holy people of the country for you."

"Rosie," said the Justice, "you have 43 previous convictions. You've been in and out of prison. You've said yourself it doesn't do you any good."

"Indeed, sir," said Rosie, "it only does me harm."

"At least prison kept you off the drink," said the Justice.

"I had to stay off it. They don't supply it there yet," riposted Rosie, with a smile.

Everyone laughed.

"Obviously prison does you no good, and I don't want to send you there if I can help it," said the Justice. "But you're a chronic alcoholic, Rosie, according to this report from St. Brendan's. I don't know whether I can let you go. What am I to do with you?"

"I don't know, sir," said Rosie. "I dread this place, I really do. I've a horror of it, the court, and I keep coming back here all the time."

"Then why do you come back?" asked the Justice.

"I can't help it. It's not me that brings me here," said Rosie.

"I will tell you what I'll do. I'll sentence you to three month's imprisonment," said the Justice. "The sentence will be suspended if you keep out of trouble for six months. Will you promise me you'll do that?"

"I'll do me best, sir," said Rosie, shuffling a well-worn path to the exit. She had promised to do her best, but she's an alcoholic and she lifts things when she's drunk and she gets caught, and she and the Justice agreed that prison does her no good at all, and now she's got a suspended sentence of three months hanging over her, which means she's got to stay out of trouble and be of good behaviour for a period longer than she's been capable of in the past.

She's got to do it on her own. In the absence of a proper welfare system in the courts. Rosie, an alcoholic with 43 convictions and nowhere permanent to stay, and who, as the guard said, doesn't really know what she's doing, has to do it on her own.

You'd get shorter odds on a three-legged horse.

1 December 1973

* * *

An old woman stumbled into the dock of Dublin District Court 4. She was dressed in a bundle of clothes and wore dark glasses. But she was sprightly enough. Indeed she did not seem at all sorry for herself; looking at her, you could even feel that such people would be happy enough if the rest of us would leave them alone, apart from extending the occasional helping hand.

District Justice Ua Donnchadha burst into a smile when he saw her. The arresting sergeant replied with a philosophic grin and a shake of the head.

"At two o'clock today, in the main street, I found the defendant sitting down with a postcard in her hand, begging. I took her into custody," he said.

"She was begging," said the Justice.

"She was begging," said the sergeant.

"Well, Rosie, do you want to ask the sergeant any questions?" the Justice addressed himself comfortably to the woman.

"No, sir," she said, "I have no questions except that I wanted the bus fare to Hyde Park Corner," she misnamed her destination.

"Look here, Rosie", said the Justice sternly, "you were here just a few hours ago. You were sitting down there in the dock. What did I do then?"

"You set me free," she said.

"And now you're back, in a matter of hours," said the Justice.

"It's been a couple of hours," she agreed.

She was not terrified; neither was she free now.

"She had a bottle of Baby Powers," said the sergeant. "And yesterday when I brought her in, she was so far gone she didn't even know her religion."

"What am I to do with you, Rosie?" asked the Justice.

"Well, sir," said Rosie, and she stopped. She knew not to ask the Justice to buy her a large bottle of whiskey; that was not what he meant.

"She has been staying out at the convent for the past three months, but on her own admission she finds the going there rather difficult," said the sergeant.

"I was out at the convent," agreed Rosie.

"Have you left the nuns?" asked the Justice.

"Only since yesterday, sir," said Rosie, skipping over her night in prison. "I'd no bus fare to go back to them this morning."

"You'd enough to get a bottle of Baby Powers," said the Justice.

"That's because people gave me the money for it," said Rosie. "But then I didn't have any more for the bus fare. My allowance is due tomorrow. I get eight pounds ten."

"What for?" asked the Justice.

"The social people," she said.

"Social welfare," said the Justice.

"There's my book," she said, taking it out of her clothes.

"I don't want to see it," said the Justice. He asked the records officer when she had been in court before, apart from that morning. The sergeant had taken the book to examine it.

"She's been all right. She hasn't been here for a while," said the records officer.

"She has an out-of-town address," said the sergeant, holding up her social welfare book.

"I left that address," said Rosie. "The social worker

got the change. I couldn't afford the rent."

"She was here in July last year," said the records officer, "She got the Probation Act. She got seven days' imprisonment in May. Then she was here in July, 1974. Then in September, 1973."

"I cannot dispense with the case without some sanction in law," said the Justice. "I can't apply the Probation Act either, having applied it some hours ago. One month's imprisonment — are you listening, Rosie? — to be suspended if you keep the peace and be of good behaviour for the next six months. That means no begging and no getting drunk. You'll hear no more about it if you keep the peace. Now it's up to you."

Rosie left the court. The matter of her bus fare remained unsettled. The convent was a long way away. The law, which allowed for her transportation to court, on a charge of begging for the fare home, did not allow for her transportation to the convent.

11 February 1976

* * *

Rosie appeared in court again, looking old but bright. She wore dark glasses and had a blue tint along the parting of her thin black hair. Her clothes were extremely clean. The same sergeant who had brought her to court before prosecuted her again. She was charged with wandering abroad and begging.

She pleaded guilty.

"I am guilty, Justice," she said. "I needed a meal and there was no other way."

"Hold on a second," said District Justice Johnston. "Let's have the facts of the case from the guard."

"I was on duty in the main street," said the sergeant, "and I observed the defendant sitting on the pavement, with a box in front of her. People going to and fro were putting money in the box."

"I needed a meal and that was the only way I could get the money," said Rosie.

"On February 4th last," said the sergeant strongly,

"she was in court in the morning for being drunk and she was brought back in the afternoon for begging. She appeared twice in one day."

"Where are you living?" asked the Justice.

"In the hostel," said Rosie.

"Have you any means to support you or what?" asked the Justice.

"Not really," said Rosie, who had told the court last time that she was in receipt of just over £8 a week pension. "There is a lunch in the hostel for six of us but you can imagine what it's like, Justice."

"The last time she was here, she said she was working in a convent," said the sergeant, who had indicated on the last occasion that Rosie had found it difficult to work in a convent.

"I don't like to do anything in this case," said the Justice. "I'll accept what she says and apply the Probation Act."

"Justice," said Rosie, "pardon me, but I'd like to go up to Mountjoy Jail for a while, for a rest. I'm very tired."

She had just spent the weekend there.

"You're a bit late," said the Justice. "I wouldn't send you to prison at any rate."

Rosie left the court, followed by the sergeant. No doubt they'll meet again, as she wends her way from convent to hostel to pavement to jail, looking for a meal there, a drink once in a while, and the odd rest.

She's a very courteous woman, in the dock. The people in the street don't have to give her money. The people in the courts say she mustn't accept it. The law under which she was prosecuted was made in 1847, and the conflict hasn't been resolved yet.

24 February 1976

Jane

A slight and sometimes smiling girl sat in the dock of Dublin District Court 6 as the prosecuting guard gave evidence to District Justice Ó hUadhaigh. Jane had been outside the American Embassy since 10 o'clock on Monday morning, the guard said, and he had finally arrested her between two and three o'clock as she tried to pull down the rope of the flag pole. She had tried to do that several times in the course of the day, and run away each time the guard approached.

The justice invited the girl to cross examine.

"I was in this court all Monday morning," the girl said firmly. "You left the court at 20 past 11, justice, and you hadn't come in till 20 minutes to 11."

"I'm not quibbling about that," said the justice. "What time did you say she appeared at the embassy, guard?"

"She appeared there after being in court," said the discomfited guard.

"I wasn't there at 10," said Jane. "Don't you remember, justice, you didn't get into court till 10 to 11, and you left at 20 past?"

"But she was at the embassy then until three?" the justice turned to the guard.

"Yes," said the guard. "Sometimes she left on the bus, when I went up to her but she'd be back five minutes later. She got off down the road at the next stop. I had to call a squad car."

"But I was in bed yesterday morning at 10," the girl persisted.

"How could she be at the embassy at 10, and in court after that, if you say she never left the embassy for more than five minutes?" the justice turned to the guard.

"I — she — that particular girl spends most of her time hanging around the embassy. She's the subject of continuous complaints from them," said the guard.

"Never mind that now," said the justice.

The girl said she pleaded guilty to trying to pull down the rope to the flag-pole, but not to the other charge. The justice explained to her that threatening, abusive, and insulting behaviour likely to lead to a breach of the peace was a charge arising out of trying to pull down the rope. He convicted.

She had a conviction in February of possession of an offensive weapon and causing malicious damage, said the guard. She had received six months' probation.

The probation officer was called to testify. "What's up with her?" asked the justice. "She's all right. I mean I got her medically examined and she's all right. This is all very unusual."

"She seems to have a fixation about the American Embassy," said the probation officer. "I can't give any explanation as to why . . . She has nothing against the Americans. She's been seen by two doctors."

"She appears to be on remand at the moment on a more serious charge," said the justice. He consulted the medical report before him, and a copy of a report furnished in a previous case. He asked the girl if she had been in a psychiatric hospital.

"That's correct, justice," she said brightly.

"She's been in jail too," said the justice.

"She was in custody for a while," said the probation officer.

"The doctors say they can't do anything with her. And you can't do anything with her?", inquired the Justice.

"In time, perhaps," said the social worker.

"In time the flag will be worn out," said the justice. All the girl's court appearances had related to the American Embassy. Her mother was called.

She was a widow, with three daughters. One worked with mentally handicapped children. The other worked with a motoring firm. This one, the youngest, used to work in a factory.

"The eldest types in the motoring place?", asked the justice.

"No, she does things for motors," said the mother. "She puts wires or something into parts of cars."

"A mechanic?", the justice's eyebrows lifted.

"I suppose you could say that," said the mother diffidently.

The justice asked her opinion of the girl before the court.

"She was in the casualty ward this morning with an accident to her shoulder," said the mother, "the time the American ambassador and his secretary were blown up."

"You mean the British ambassador," said the justice.

"Well, they were blown up in a car and she was there when they were brought into hospital. Soon after that she started ringing the American Embassy and I've never had a minute's peace since."

The doctors seemed to be useless, the woman continued. "She says they only ever examine her chest, and it's her head needs examined." The justice opined that the girl was mistaken about what the doctors did, although "psychiatrists are entitled to examine her chest if they want to, though I doubt if they would."

"There's something radically wrong with her," said the mother. "I wonder if it's the uniform that attracts her. She applied to join the police in England."

The girl smiled.

"It's not funny," the mother turned to her. "I work as well, justice, four hours every morning, and I can't keep coming down to court. She mostly appears in court in the morning. But she doesn't want to be put away in jail. She's looking forward to her Easter eggs."

"She's too big for Easter eggs. Eggs are for children," said the justice, who can't have been near the department stores this year, and I hope my mother isn't reading this, because she gives me a big one every Easter.

"I can't keep her in chains; that's one thing. I can't bring her to work with me on a rope. That's my honest opinion anyway. You can take it or leave it."

The girl said she lost two jobs already, because of the embassy business, and got £9.50 a week pay-related benefit. She gave her mother five pounds out of that.

"What do you do with the rest. Do you spend it on sweets?", asked the justice.

"I don't know where it disappears to . . . bus fares," worried the girl.

"I hear they're very dear now," agreed the justice. He consulted his papers. "I'm satisfied from this report that you're fit to plead," he said. "But I don't see how one doctor can say that, and the other says you have the mentality of a ten-year-old. You can't blow hot and cold on these matters. You seem to be either mentally deranged or childish." However, the American Embassy and personnel were entitled to protection, "though I daresay if they saw you they wouldn't be too upset."

He bound her to keep the peace, and stressed that she would need an independent bonds person, other than her mother. "You've been dealt with leniently before this," he warned. "I may as well tell you I would have sent you to jail if you'd appeared on a more serious charge, but I can't do that on this one. According to the psychiatrists, you should be locked up."

The girl left the dock, smiling.

6 April 1977

* * *

Jane's name was called but she did not appear in the dock. "She won't come upstairs, I understand," the clerk of Dublin District Court 6 remarked to District Justice Ó hUadhaigh. "Ah, she will," said the Justice. Down below in the holding cells the guards were trying to coax the seventeen-year-old girl who had already been convicted several times of interfering with the property of the American Embassy.

A guard came up the stairs and into the dock. "My application is for a remand for a week. She won't come up. She's kicking up a racket," he said.

"Hold on there. There's more to it than that," said the justice, with due regard for the process of law. "Go back down and talk to her. Maybe she'll come up when the court is empty. Give her a cup of tea or something. There's her mother. She can go down and talk to her," he indicated the woman hovering at the side. "Or maybe she won't talk to you after yesterday?" he queried the woman.

"Jane," the woman leaned over the railing of the dock calling down to the cells.

"Go down and see her," the justice said. The woman disappeared down the stairs.

Another case was called, and as the defendant entered the dock, the girl appeared at the top of the stairs, her arms lightly pinioned to her sides by two guards. They saw that they had missed their chance and led her back down again. The mother came up and went to sit in the public gallery.

An hour later the clerk called the girl's case again. The guards looked warily at him. "She had to be called at some stage," the clerk said. The guards went below. There were words heard and some slight noise. The girl came up the stairs, her right arm firmly pinioned behind her by a guard. She took her place in the dock.

"Close the door," the clerk indicated the half-door leading to the stairs of the holding cells. It was closed, she was in place, and the case commenced.

A guard testified that between seven and eight p.m., some weeks ago, he had arrested the girl outside the American Embassy. The charge was one of malicious damage to the rope of the flag-pole. "Do you want free legal aid?" the justice asked her. She did. The Justice assigned a solicitor who was sitting on the bench. The solicitor had appeared for her before. A remand was granted.

Another guard took the oath. He had arrested the girl in the early hours of Wednesday morning, between one and two a.m., outside the Swedish Embassy. She was charged with possession of a key to the Embassy. The justice asked her if she wanted free legal aid. She did, and the same solicitor was assigned to her.

The guard asked for remand in custody for a week, because she had failed to turn up for a previous hearing, when remanded in her own bail. The solicitor rose to his feet with a murmur.

"I have to have medical and psychiatric reports on her," the justice said. "Look here, Mister Solicitor, this child, or woman or whatever she is, an adult, she was before the court twice on Monday, once on Tuesday and now again today. She doesn't appear to me to be the full shilling. I have to have reports on her. She failed to turn up once before. Remand in custody for a week."

The solicitor asked that the representatives of the two Embassies and the doctors who examined her be in court on that occasion. The justice agreed.

The girl did not smile at all, as she had done on Tuesday

when convicted of trying to pull down the flag-pole rope of the American Embassy. Her mother, who had lost another morning's work, did not repeat her Tuesday plea that she be not "put away," if only that she be free to eat her Easter eggs. The guard who had arrested the girl outside the Swedish Embassy ten hours after her conviction in connection with the American Embassy, smiled at the girl quite hopelessly as he led her back down below.

7 April 1977

John

A tall, thin man, red-haired, open-mouthed and amiable, came up from the cells below. His shirt was open to the waist, and blood-stained. His left trouser leg was torn from the thigh down, and his trousers fly was unzipped and open. The Justice said to him: "The chief clerk has handed me your letter asking for assault charges against the gardai. We can't decipher the numbers. They mean nothing anyway without a letter in front." "There were letters," said the man. "Well, there's a 'D' and an 'A'," said the Justice, "what about the others?" John said he didn't know.

The Justice said he was only trying to deal with the letter before him. "I think I did advise you last time that if you wish to complain and issue a summons against the gardai, you need both the number and the letter. I can't issue a summons against a number one hundred. There is no such garda."

"I beg your pardon," said the defendant. "There is, he's right here in court." He would issue summonses against those numbered and lettered in the letter, said the Justice. The defendant then complained that he had been remanded five or six times. "Well, you didn't appear well last time you were in court," said the Justice.

"If you're going to remand me again", said the defendant, "how about a full psychiatric report?" "You asked for a medical report, and you got it; there's nothing wrong with you," said the Justice. "You mightn't think so," said the defendant, "but there's others would disagree with you. I need a full report. I desperately need one."

"You look alright to me," said Justice Ó hUadhaigh: "You don't need a psychiatrist. I'm only a lay-man, but you seem reasonable to me, you know your rights, anyway. You look alright to me. I'm remanding you to March 5th. There's bail on you, anyway."

"Ah, who'd bail me out, for Jesus' sake," said the man going back down to the cells.

28 February 1973

* * *

The man in torn trousers, open fly and blood-stained shirt, turned up again in a similar state in Dublin District Court No. 4 yesterday, before Justice Ó hUadhaigh. He was still in custody, unable to get bail, and he objected to his case being remanded once more. He was still demanding psychiatric treatment, and he told Justice Ó hUadhaigh that he had been before the High Court last Friday to discuss bail and his demand for proper treatment. He referred to himself in the third person.

"A man went up before his high worship last Friday," he told Justice Ó hUadhaigh, "and he told me to come down and speak with you this time. Now a man is destitute, and because he has nobody belonging to him to help him get bail and things like that, the man is destitute. I do need psychological help, your honour."

"Wait a minute," said Justice Ó hUadhaigh, "you did get a medical report."

"Ah, he said I was physically fit," John said.

"He said you were fit to plead," said the Justice.

"But look at the nature of the charge," said the man. "I'm asking for Grangegorman Hospital. A man can't get bail, and he does seriously need looking after."

"I don't like referring to this," said the Justice, "but I saw you here before, and you gave the impression of being violent. I used the phrase towards you that I thought you were putting on a bit of an act. The gardai had to hold you down. Anyway, the doctor says you're fit to plead."

"Would you not send me to the Grange for a bit,"

123

the man said. "A man could be a long time without bail if a man is destitute."

"Now look," said the Justice, "forget for a minute that you've no people or anything. I have no power to send you anywhere. With the best will in the world there's nothing I can do. The doctor says you're fit. All I can decide is if you've a case to answer or not."

"But I've been a long time on remand," said the man.

"I know that," said the Justice, and he turned on the prosecutor, who had asked for another week. "What's the delay? This is a straight case of buggery. I've done 25 or 50 charges myself in my day. It's straightforward. I'm making a peremptory remand for this day week. If you're not ready this man can walk out of my court. The responsibility lies on the shoulders of the Attorney-General. If you're not ready, I'll tell this man to walk out a free man."

6 March 1973

* * *

As a result of the fact that the State prosecution had stated that it was not yet ready to go ahead with the case, a man accused of buggery, larceny and assaulting the gardai was told by District Justice Ó hUadhaigh yesterday to leave the court a free man.

Yesterday, the State solicitor, in Dublin District Court 4, told Justice Ó hUadhaigh that the book of evidence was not ready yet, but it had been prepared and he requested a further remand. The man said then: "Your honour, you promised me you'd let me out if they couldn't go ahead today".

"I didn't promise you anything", said the justice.

"Yes, you did," said John.

The book of evidence had been ready for "some few days", the State solicitor said, but it had not yet been typed out.

"We can't have that sort of thing," the justice said. "You say you've had the book ready for some few days. What exactly do you mean by some few days? Why wasn't it typed out? I marked this case peremptory last week, the man has been in custody since last January, he can't get bail, he's entitled to have his case heard — what about the other charges? There's assault against the gardai, and larceny — can you go ahead with them?"

"We can have one book ready by Thursday", the State said.

"One book?", the justice asked. "Only one book ready? The charges are straightforward. They're simple. Buggery's a simple straightforward case, and you've had him since January? The scales must be weighed reasonably, you know."

"Well, Justice," said the State, "in view of the allegations before the court . . . the nature of the charges . . ."

"If it was murder, it would be the same thing," the justice said.

"I'm going to ask for a remand until Thursday", the State finished.

"Well, I'm refusing it," the justice said. "He's been in custody too long. Go on, you can go. Get out of here," he said to the defendant.

"Thank you, your honour. Thanks, Justice," said the man, amiably.

"You needn't thank me," said the justice.

"Well, I'm thanking you," said the man, "you gave me a fair deal, you're the only one gave me a fair deal. Thanks again," he shouted, as he walked out the door of the court.

13 March 1973

* * *

After several weeks in custody, the district justice finally dismissed the charges because of the State's unreasonable delay in prosecuting the case.

Yesterday John appeared in Court again, on charges of indecently assaulting two boys within the last week. He was convicted on the unsworn testimony of the minors concerned. In the course of the hearing, District Justice Good asked one of the boys why he had not told his

125

father what the man had been doing to them, and referred to "these dirty actions." The man himself denied the charges.

He had several previous convictions for similar offences in Australia, the Court was told, for which he received three years' hard labour, and suspended sentences on condition that he receive medical treatment. He was deported from Australia last year.

He then received a prison sentence in Dublin last year for a similar offence. Justice Good told the man that he was obviously "some kind of a pervert", and he put him back for a week for sentencing, while he awaits a medical report.

4 July 1973

* * *

Now, District Justice Good told the man in Dublin District Court 4, he had the report before him. "I think you really need some treatment," said the justice. "Are you prepared to attend a doctor?" The man said that he would be prepared to do this. "I'm worried about your health. The report suggests you need help, and you can avail of that help if you place yourself under the control of the probation officer . . . you do need some treatment, with all respect . . . . I propose to put you under rule of bail, under the supervision of the probation officer."

"That's fair enough," said John, who had served several jail terms in Australia for similar offences. The justice made the order, adding as a condition of bail that the man was not to associate with anyone under the age of 17. The man went out to sign his bail bond, and when he returned to court the justice called him up to the bench, and they had a few quiet words together. "Do you feel happy with the order?" the justice asked the man. "Well, I thought I might be scared to come up this high, to your bench," said the man, "but I'm grateful for the chance for treatment." He told the justice that he didn't know if he could stay out of the Court's way for a full year, "but I'll try," he said. "I'll try. I may be back here another 55 times, and another 55 times after that, but I'll certainly try. I just want you to know that."

They smiled at each other, and the justice said something in a low voice, and the man replied, and then they shook hands. "I've found you the best of all judges I've met from here to Australia," said the man as he stepped down from the bench. "You're the best of all, your honour, and that's not crawling to you to say it. It's true."

11 July 1973

Chapter 9
Religion & Politics

"They were walking down Grafton Street playing music and making a lot of noise. I had cautioned them on previous occasions not to play music to the annoyance of the inhabitants of the street. There have been serious complaints from the inhabitants, and they were making considerable noise. They were using cymbals and drums and bells. They were walking in single file but people had to walk in the roadway to avoid them." The detective concluded his evidence before District Justice Breathnach in Dublin District Court 6.

The five accused people stood gentle and smiling before the District Justice. All of them were dressed in the now familiar pink, yellow and orange cotton robes of the Hare Krishna religious sect. Their heads were entirely shaven, except for a short thin strand of pigtail growing from the backs of their skulls. Each had a pink cotton purse hanging from his wrist, in which were the beads which they constantly fingered as they prayed. One boy disengaged himself from the proceedings and meditated happily, his lips fervently moving.

His companion, the only one to wear a cloth over his head, had a cylindrical drum suspended from his neck, to which was attached the musical bells beloved of Orientals. The bells tinkled musically as he shifted his feet. "Will you keep that thing quiet please?" snapped the District Justice. "Take it off, take it off," commanded the court sergeant.

A brown-eyed youth studied the charges of the sheet in his hand. They had been collectively accused of "using noisy instruments, to wit, cymbals and drums for the purpose of distributing literature relating to a religious sect for the purpose of gathering people together."

They were also accused of "committing an offence — to wit, marching in single file, playing instruments, and obstructing traffic."

They were finally accused of "insulting behaviour, whereby a breach of the peace may be occasioned."

We weren't obstructing traffic, the brown-eyed youth said. Did they want to question the guard's evidence? the District Justice asked. There was silence, and the District Justice asked the detective if they understood what he was saying.

"Do they speak English?" the District Justice asked uneasily. "Oh yes, one comes from Wales, one from Trinidad, and the other three from Ireland," said the detective. They said they didn't want to question the detective, but would like to defend themselves, without taking the oath. "I'll just give my evidence from here, is that all right?" asked the boy. That was all right.

"Well, as far as the charges go," the first said, "to draw people together and distribute literature. Now nobody distributed literature. And we didn't get in anybody's way. We have been charged before, and the justice told us last time that we should march in single file and not obstruct the highway, and that's what we did."

"That's what the sergeant says, you obstructed traffic," said the district justice. "Oh no, we didn't, we marched in single file along the gutter," said the boy. "We were simply walking along the side of the footpath, in single file, not getting in anybody's way, as far as I could see. There were not too many people around at the time. Nobody had to walk in the road."

The others reiterated his evidence, and the boy from Wales said he had done this all over world and no one had ever told him before that he was not allowed to do this.

The district justice said he was satisfied they were

guilty as charged. "Why are you dressed up in those ridiculous garments?" the district justice then burst out. "We are monks," the brown-eyed boy explained. "I could sentence you for contempt, wearing a scarf in Court like that," the district justice said.

"I understand they're a religious sect," the detective explained, "though of course I've no objection to them as such, it's just that they were playing instruments and collecting." (That was the first we'd heard of collecting).

"I can warn you that you are lucky not to have been assaulted by a crowd. Any decent Irishman would object to this carry-on," District Justice Breathnach told these members of a religious sect, which differs from the religion of the vast majority of Irishmen. (Does that mean that those of us who do not object are not decent? Or will a sympathetic view now be taken by the Courts of those Catholic Irishmen who take it upon themselves to tear the Hare Krishna members limb from limb?)

"They were warned on previous occasions to desist from this behaviour," the detective said, restraining his sense of outrage.

"I've no jurisdiction to order a forfeiture of those things, bells and leaflets. If I had, I'd be fairly radical and confiscate those nonsensical things," said the district justice.

"Why do you say nonsensical?" asked the brown-eyed boy.

"Because you're disturbing the peace of this city, and I'm sure my colleagues will agree with my only regret that I can't have you locked up," said the district justice.

"May I say something about our movement?" asked the boy.

"I don't want to hear anything about your movement, whether you keep stationary or not," said the district justice cleverly.

He then fined them a total of seven pounds each on all the charges. "I can tell you," finished the district justice, "that the only reason I'm not imposing heavier fines is that I don't have the jurisdiction . . . though I suppose I could increase the fine for obstructing the traffic and playing those instruments."

Christian charity prevailed, however, and he let them go.

The monks stood out in the courtyard afterwards, and some of the gardai asked them for their leaflets. One guard asked them to play him a tune, remarking to me that "they had drink and sex and everything in the houses where they lived."

Another guard asked them why they wore those ridiculous clothes, which made them stand out. The boy pointed out that the guard's uniform was equally conspicuous, and the guard said that he was paid to wear it. The boy pointed out that nuns and priests wore distinctive habits also, and the guard said they led good lives.

"I mean look at that boy over there praying against a wall," said the guard, pointing to the monk who was meditating. "What's wrong with praying?" asked the boy. "You should pray in the church," said the guard, "and anyway the priests aren't praying all day."

Earlier District Justice Breathnach had fined a travelling woman, who appeared in Court with her baby swaddled in a blanket, charged with begging. The woman's husband was in jail. "This is the tourist season," said the district justice, "and it makes a bad impression on them to go back to their own countries with memories of having been accosted on the streets. They'll think we're a nation of beggars."

That must be it. First, the Maoists; then the travelling people, now the monks of Hare Krishna — bring them into Court and off the streets — keep Ireland Catholic and clean for the tourists. They'll be puttin' a curfew on Benburb Street next. (I wonder what will happen the Dublin shops which sell coloured cotton robes and musical bells?)

As I crossed the bridge after the Court session I passed a shabbily-dressed blind man playing a flute. Trying to be decent and in the majority I restrained myself from throwing him over the bridge and into the Liffey. Luckily there were no tourists about.

9 June 1973

Dissidents

"Stand up in Court," the sergeant called as District Justice Ó hUadhaigh entered Dublin District Court 6. The district justice was about to seat himself when the sergeant called out again, "stand up in Court, you." The man at the back, who had just been released after serving seven days for contempt, remained seated. Then he raised himself a little, and the district justice lowered himself a little. "Stand up," the sergeant called again and the man continued raising himself off his bench, as the district justice proportionately lowered himself onto his chair. Bottoms poised in mid-air as the stage tensed. Finally, the man got up and the district justice got down. Law and order was restored.

The man came forward then to answer charges. A member of the Communist Party of Ireland, Marxist Leninist, he was charged with selling literature without a street-trader's licence, with assaulting the gardai, resisting arrest, and obstructing the police in the due execution of their duty. The man had twice been sentenced for contempt of Court, because he persisted in asking the gardai why they had charged him with breaking a law, when none of the public, the man alleged, objected to his selling literature, and indeed bought it off him.

"There's no need to repeat the evidence," the garda began. "Why not, I haven't cross-questioned yet," the man replied. His Maoist badge was prominent on his lapel. "Before you begin", District Justice Ó hUadhaigh warned him, "I can tell you here and now that the only questions allowed are those relevant to the issue."

"That's what's been going on since I came before this Court," the man said. "I have to put up with this sort of thing every time I'm brought here." "Do you intend to address the Court now on the evidence, or continue questioning?" asked the district justice. "If you want to ask questions, cease the preliminaries and get on with it, please." "The conduct of this trial is in flagrant breach of your own laws. My arguments expose the nature of this Court," the defendant said.

"If you continue like this, I'll have to take a certain

course," the district justice said. "I'm going to question this lackey here," the man said, pointing to the garda. "Kindly stop that. If you proceed in this manner, I'll have you removed to the cells, and continue the case in your absence," the district justice said.

"Fine," said the man. "That exposes the nature of this Court even further." The district justice ordered the gardai to remove him. A garda took the man by the shoulder, he called out "down with Fascism" and pulled away. Another garda caught him, and again he called "down with Fascism," and his arms were outstretched now, his feet spreadeagled. Two more gardai grabbed him and he was taken down the steps to the cells below. There was much noise, and sounds came thumping off the wooden stairway, and then up from the cells came a cry "get off him, get off him, leave him alone." Struggling thumping sounds, and the cry "down with Fascism."

The Court waited in silence, and the cries and noises came echoing up: "Leave him alone, leave him alone, down with Fascism, leave him alone, leave him alone." The noises ceased. The Court resumed its deliberations. A police inspector told how he had tried to reason with the defendant on the occasion of his arrest in Thomas Street, only to be told that he was 'arrogant'. The man refused to give his name and address and the sergeant had put his hand on his shoulder.

The man had said: "You will not arrest me," had put his hands on his head and called on passers-by to help him "resist the Fascists". There was a struggle and he and his companion were put into the patrol car.

The inspector produced the literature which was being unlawfully sold, and the solicitor asked with a smile if these books were copies of "The Thoughts of Chairman Mao"; the inspector agreed with a smile that they were, and the other gardai involved in the case also smiled. At this point the Court sergeant went to the back of the Court and asked a member of the public to remove his feet from the bench in front of him.

All was present and correct, and the district justice proceeded to enunciate his thoughts. "Well, we'll have to have

133

that man brought up again, in fairness to him. I think, Court sergeant, if you're of the opinion that he will continue to behave in the manner just exhibited, you may come back and tell me. I don't want the performance of 10 minutes ago. If you're of the opinion that there will be difficulty getting him up the stairs, you can tell me."

The sergeant disappeared down below and the cry came up "down with Fascism" and the sergeant came back up to report that "this man will probably take whatever course he wants to."

The district justice observed that the defendant had, by his own actions, waived his right to a normal trial, and he convicted him. The garda said that the defendant had no actual previous convictions. He had been charged once with an offence under the Public Meetings Act, had been committed for seven days for contempt and the case had not proceeded to conviction. The only other thing he knew was that the defendant had given his occupation as "Rat-catcher, though I find that rather hard to believe, Justice." "I know what he means," the district justice remarked.

District Justice Ó hUadhaigh said that anyone was entitled to expound political views, provided they were expounded within the laws of the State, but in his opinion this defendant had transgressed the law in order to be arrested and appear in Court, thereby getting himself cheap publicity, by the manner in which he behaved in Court. Well now he couldn't be allowed to do this at the expense of the citizens, and the gardai had presented their evidence fairly, and he had no reason to disbelieve them. "Unfortunately for the defendant, or maybe fortunately for him, this is a serious offence, meriting severe punishment," and violence against the gardai was endemic — obstructing, resisting and assaulting them for reasons which the district justice found mostly "to be pure figments of the imagination."

The district justice could not tolerate attacks on "the unarmed forces of the State," and he sentenced the man to six months' imprisonment and indeed if the man had had previous convictions, the district justice said, he would have given him 12 months. (The man's companion had been fined £12 by District Justice Coglan, two weeks ago, for the same offences. District Justice Ó hUadhaigh was out of the city that day.)

The next case involved a member of the same political party who had been, the garda testified, "distributing pamphlets outside the G.P.O., carrying a red book, and obstructing the path of passers-by." (The man first appeared on this charge six weeks ago; he had then pleaded "not guilty to crimes against the Irish people" and opposed the right of the Court to try him, and was subsequently given seven days for contempt by District Justice O hUadhaigh.)

The man had refused to move on when asked, the garda said, and had refused to give his name and address. The garda had then arrested him. When the garda placed his hand on his shoulder, the man had "turned round, hit me on the body, caught hold of me, and when I held him on the ground had violently resisted me, and tried to incite a hostile crowd to resist the fascists and the imperialist Government."

The man asked the garda why he and his companion had been singled out from among the many groups of people selling or distributing literature outside the G.P.O. that Saturday, and the garda replied: "Most of them gave their names and addresses or had licences." "Why wasn't I arrested the following week when I was there again?" the man asked, and the garda said "I didn't see you."

"I put it to you," said the man, "that this was part of a three-pronged Government plan to attack us, on three different occasions, at Westland Row, at the G.P.O. and in Thomas Street — in order to wipe out, intimidate us and prevent the sale of revolutionary literature." "I couldn't say that," said the garda. "You mean you can't, said the man. "This is an ordinary garda" said the district justice. "He's a Fascist", said the man. "That is contempt", said the district justice. "This is intimidation," said the man. The garda admitted that the crowd was hostile to the police and had said things like "traitors" and "bastards."

"Do you claim to protect the people's rights therefore?" asked the man. The district justice said the garda didn't claim this, but was only enforcing the law and he didn't have to answer the question. "You mean he's no mind of his own?" asked the man. There followed an exchange between the district justice and the man, with the district justice saying he wasn't going to bandy words, and that "Communist, Fascist, Nazi or democratic attack is not the issue here."

"It's the Fascists who attack", said the man, "we are Communists."

When another garda was questioned by the man about the attitude of the crowd which had gathered round, the district justice said that it was already proved that the crowd was hostile to the police, and the man said "so that proves we stand for the rights of the people."

The defendant then addressed the district justice, basing his right to sell or distribute literature on his political right to alert the people to imperialism and economic discrimination of the working class North and South. The district justice stopped him eventually, pointing out that it was normal practice to allow such speeches in Court only to people who were under sentence of death — and then only after sentence and conviction had been pronounced.

There were no previous convictions against the man, the garda said, but the district justice remarked that he felt himself that the man had been before him on a previous occasion. The whole thing was serious, the district justice thought, the "unlawful circulation of propaganda by way of street-trading" and the attack on and resistance and obstruction of the police, and he sentenced the man to six months in prison.

"Death to British Imperialism", called the man as they led him below. "Long live the Communist Party of Ireland, Marxist Leninist."

25 May 1973

Liberty and licensing

The list of defendants read like a Who's Who of the political party they belonged to: Official Sinn Fein. The State was prosecuting them. As they gathered in Dublin District Court 1 you could look out the window and see the bullet marks on the pillars of the Four Courts, recalling another battle, long ago, between the forces of the State and those who would oppose it.

District Justice Donnelly regarded the parties impartially. He refused an adjournment of the battle, on the sympathetic grounds that the defendants couldn't afford to be taking days off work. "All of them must be working?" he asked rhetorically, looking at the revolutionary faces ranged before him. "Most of them?" he qualified himself. "Some of them?" he faltered.

An inspector took the witness stand and told the justice how he had entered the premises of the political party concerned, on foot of a warrant. He knocked at the basement door and was admitted by a man "whom I told about the purpose of my visit, that I had a warrant to enter the place and search it for liquor. I told him of the powers invested in me: to seize all liquor on the premises and arrest the persons who refused to give me their names and addresses.

"There were 40 or 50 persons sitting at tables, on which there was a collection of assorted drinks – beer, stout and short drinks. As I had gone in the door, through a little lounge sort of place, I saw barrels of beer and drink dispensers and a till, and a service hatch. There was somebody at the service hatch."

The inspector then produced his exhibits. Cardboard sheets on which were printed, in Irish, the various drinks and their prices.

The justice reviewed the lists. "Twenty-one pence a pint?" he asked.

"And here's another list in English," said the inspector. The justice reviewed it. It was written in Irish, he pointed out. The inspector apologised. (Irish is no longer required for certain Government positions).

The inspector read out the names of the beverages. . . Guinness, Smithwicks, Winter's Tale sherry, Babycham, Snowball, six sorts of whiskey and some very good brandy, Martini and Dubonnet.

A comprehensive list at competitive prices.

One of the women present had accompanied him to the station to oversee the enumeration of the drink, a sample of which the inspector now produced in court. Bottles and bottles of it.

The justice asked the defendants if any of them wished to cross-examine the inspector. "I don't even know where the place is. I'm 76 years of age and I wasn't there," called out a peeved defendant.

"I gather," said the inspector, "that his name was given falsely to us."

A sergeant then testified that the premises were not registered as a drinking club. He had interviewed a man who had rented the basement from the landlord of the building.

The justice invited cross-examination by the defendants. He observed that summonses had not been served in respect of some of the defendants named in the charge. He noted the name of one such defendant, Paddy Murphy, and remarked with a smile that of course no person by such a name could exist. A standard alias in troubled times.

The peeved 76-year-old again insisted that he had never been near the place. His wife vociferously backed him up. A guard testified that all the drinkers had been youthful, and the justice dismissed charges against the old man.

"I hope you haven't lost anything by coming here today," said the justice. "In any case there's nothing I can do if you have. You may however have gained an interesting experience. You can write about it in your memoirs. 'The night I was not found in a shebeen'."

Exit the man and his wife.

The landlord was called. Had he rented his basement to the person named in the charge? the State prosecutor asked. The justice observed that this person was the subject of a criminal charge, and that the landlord therefore should not be led in questioning. He must make his own statement freely.

Were the premises rented? asked the State.

They were, said the landlord.

To whom? asked the State.

To the person named in the charge, said the landlord.

Could he point out this person in court? asked the State.

The landlord looked around. The person waved. "Ah, John," said the landlord with a smile, and pointed a cheerfully incriminating finger at John.

The State rested its case.

John's defence solicitor pointed out that John had not been in the basement that night. He had merely rented the premises for purposes of running a cultural Irish club. The man who had let the inspector into the premises had been accepting responsibility only for the people therein, not for the drink. The woman who accompanied the inspector to the station had merely gone along to keep an eye on things.

John, suggested the justice, had had to face a *prima facie* case of keeping the premises for the sale of drink.

As to the second charge against the man and woman who had spoken to and accompanied the inspector, respectively, the justice found the parsing and analysis of the charge to constitute an offence against the English language, rather than constitute a charge in itself. He professed not to understand it. But then, he pointed out, he had never heard a case before connected with drinking on unlicensed premises.

The State asked the justice to amend the charge. The justice said it was a bad day to ask for a charge to be amended on grammatical grounds. The State referred to the woman as "Smith," and the justice gently reminded him that all defendants were entitled to the prefix Mr., Mrs., or Miss.

"The lady Smith," the State amended. Shades of Countess Markievicz.

The justice dismissed charges against the lady Smith. She was warmly congratulated by her co-defendants.

Another victory over the State.

The defence solicitor said he did not wish to call his other clients in evidence. He would stand or fall on the justice's decision on the evidence so far adduced against John and the man who had let the inspector in. The justice convicted.

He advised the unrepresented defendants of their rights and pointed out that they could get off if they swore that they had not been consuming liquor and had no intention of consuming liquor, or that they did not know the premises to be unlicensed.

At this point Paddy Murphy stood up. "I am Paddy Murphy," he announced. The justice did a double-take. "I thought you didn't exist," he said.

"I am Paddy Murphy," said Paddy Murphy, "and I don't even drink. I only take Cidona, which is not intoxicating, I got a summons for drinking Cidona."

"Well, the summons is not returned as served," said the justice, "and that being so, you are under no liability and you can go home if you want."

Exit Paddy Murphy.

Two girls who had gone away on holiday were represented by their parents. "My daughter told me she thought the place was licensed," said the mother. The justice regretted that the girl would have to swear to that personally.

"This is my girl's first demeanour," said a father.

Both girls were fined £3.

The other drinkers were fined £8.

John was fined £30 for keeping a premises for the sale of drink, and £20 for being the occupier of the premises. The man who let the inspector in was fined £15.

The justice gave them all two months to pay, to save paper-work for the secretaries in that all summonses for non-payment could be sent out on the one day.

The State applied for an order for forfeiture of the drink. There was £700 worth in all. The defence solicitor said that proceedings had been instituted to regularise the position of the cultural club.

The justice refused to make a snap decision on £700

worth of drink, and adjourned the matter for a week to enable all concerned to study the relevant statute.

Some of the drink was going bad, said the State. And some of it was improving with age, said the inspector.

The case, which lasted an hour and 40 minutes, closed at 5.05. Different times, different battles.

5 June 1975

Chapter 10
Crime Wave

The stockings hung in thick cream wreaths around her legs; no flesh to cling to on those old bones. Her face wrinkled in ancient curiosity around her still glasses, under a black hat. A flowered dress, in winter, under a cloth coat, and a woollen scarf. She was an old-age pensioner, and her handbag containing a pension book and £4.29, of which £3.50 was in 50p pieces wrapped in a handkerchief, had been stolen, the garda told Justice Good. He had apprehended the defendant in a pub, and he was here now in Dublin District Court No. 6 to answer charges.

She was far too old to climb the stairs to the witness box, so the Justice ordered that she be questioned while seated on the solicitor's bench before and below him.

Can you hear me, the garda asked her loudly. "Oh, I can hear, thank God", she said with vigour, surprised at his tone. She commenced a conversational answer to his questions; this lady who was no dozer.

"Were you in your house on the night of January 9th around eight o'clock?"

"Oh. I'm always in the house . . . yes I left my flat for a while. I left the door open, but I left me money in the bag, and then the bag was gone . . . the bag was beside me, always beside me bed, or the other place where I get the grub from . . . I left the flat for a second or two, and the bag there . . . be God sure I thought there was no one there . . . he took me book and money . . . he likes the money, he's not a bad fella, he's (here she pointed to her head, in a screwing motion) . . . I had old money, you know the old money, and new money in a tin box".

Did I give him permission? No, hardly. No indeed. What do you mean did I give him permission?

The garda asked her to look at the defendant behind her.

"Ooohhh, he's behind me, oh be God, he's behind me?"

Do you know this man, the garda asked her.

"Ah yes, I know him. He's not bad, he's very nice". She refused to look behind her, and the defendant came to her side, at the edge of the bench.

"Ah, there he is, yeah, he's very nice right enough . . . how're ya . . . he had a flat in the same house as myself, he's gone now, he has a nice wife . . . he had a couple on him, sure he didn't know what he was doin', I feel sorry for him, he's good in his own way, he has a new house now and a job . . . oh, I'm all alone, all mine are dead and buried."

The defendant spoke then. "First of all, Justice, may I say I find it very distressin' for her to appear in this condition. If you don't mind, I'll call her Mary, I've always called her Mary . . . Mary . . ."

She said: "Yes, dear, what is it?"

"Do you see me Mary, I'm behind you. You know we left on Thursday and moved to Inchicore. Jean left me to go back and see her relatives. She didn't like it out there . . . Mary, did you see me do anything wrong? Answer me question, Mary, just the once, has there been robberies, and gas meters busted, and the phone box too in the house? Weren't we always complaining?"

Mary told the Justice then that her bag had been found in the middle of the road. The missing keys were the only thing she minded, the keys to her flat. She had no water, and there was darkness, and a fella helped her. The defendant took the witness box to give his story.

"The Thursday previous we left our furnished flat. We'd been there seven years and finally broke through to a Corporation house. Unfortunately my wife is highly strung, and she said she didn't like it there and walked out.

I told her it was like Buckingham Palace compared to a dungeon; the new house is very nice by the way. She walked out on me, and I guessed she was away back to her sisters.

"On Saturday I went looking for her. She wasn't with her relatives, and it occurred to me she'd be away back to the old flat, though it was very depressing. I was working Saturday, and I went there on Saturday night between seven and eight. Miss Smith here lived above us, up the stairs. At this point — I must tell you she's a very bad sleeper, that's important, she always takes a sleep late in the evening, after her tea, she hates to be disturbed then. At eleven at night I would bring her up a cup of tea with a biscuit and a smoke, me or my wife, and in winter I'd light the fire for her (Mary was nodding her head at this). She has no one but the Vincent de Paul. The wife's place was in darkness. It occurred to me she might come back late, so I came out of the house and found the pension book on the tenement steps. I knew instinctively it was Mary's. There's only one old person in the house. I was going to go straight back up, but I knew she was sleeping, and I'd be coming back later that evening, so I kept the book for safe-keeping, and went to the pub and had a pint and looked at TV. I received a tap on the shoulder, it was the guard, I was taken outside and searched . . ."

In answer to the garda's question, the defendant said: "I normally keep my money in a hankie, the material in trousers pockets is flimsy. I've lost money before like that. I distribute it evenly over all my pockets instead of the one."

Beckett, thou shouldst be with us at this hour!

The man stood up in the witness box and pulled out the lining of his trousers pocket to show the Justice. It was newly sewn. He pushed his fingers through holes in the pockets of his working-man's jacket and wiggled them at the Justice, sincerely.

"I had a steady job and a new life open to me. I had no reason to steal from this old lady . . . excuse me, Justice, there were also two-shilling pieces, as well as ten-shilling pieces, in me hankie. I was searched out on the pavement, like on the TV and films. Very unpleasant it was."

"I am satisfied," said Justice Good, "that you took and stole the money. You took advantage of this old lady. You are a very plausible thief. There's not one solitary grain of truth in what you've told me."

The man had two previous convictions, the garda told the court. In February, 1972, he had received the Probation of Offenders Act for assault and breach of the peace. In September, 1972, he got a six-month suspended sentence for burglary and malicious damage.

"You're a mean, contemptible despicable thief," said Justice Good. "You took advantage of this old lady, and bent so low as to steal a handbag from this old lady for a few shillings. I sentence you to nine months' imprisonment. Appeal bail fixed at self in £20 and two independent sureties of £100. Take him away."

"Oh God," said Mary, putting her head in her hands.

8 February 1973

Constructive burglary

"A knock came to the door, around eleven at night, and I said 'Who's there?'. I had the chain on the door and the lock bolted," she told District Justice Ua Donnchadha in Dublin District Court 4.

"He said: 'It's Kevin' (Kevin's his brother) and I opened the door, foolishly, I know that, I pulled back the latch and the chain and he pushed the door in and he locked it behind him.

"I pushed the door, of course, back at him, but he was stronger than me."

"Who was? You must identify him," said the Justice.

"Him there, the accused, Kevin's brother. Kevin works for us, he does odd jobs and cleans windows. The accused had come to me that morning looking for work too, but I had nothing for him, and he came back at night . . . He told me not to scream and make no noise, he had me petrified. He talked about his brother's bicycle being stolen, and I hadn't any money, and he said that there was plenty in the house.

"Then he saw my sister making for the back door: Evelyn, going to alert the neighbours, and he pushed her back and locked the kitchen door.

"He saw my purse on the table and I said 'All right,' I would give him money, and Evelyn would give him a pound too, and he said that that was no use. Then he took Winnie's my other sister's bag, and he took the wallet out."

"When he took the wallet did you know what it contained," asked the Justice. "Oh, yes, £23. Winnie told me after."

"But is that lady here now," asked the Justice. "No, she's got a medical condition, your honour," said the detective. "She's 84," said the woman.

"I can't admit evidence on hearsay, you see," explained the Justice. "In other words, did you know of your own knowledge how much the wallet contained?" "No," said the woman. "Then I can't admit it in evidence," said the Justice.

"Did you see money in the wallet?" asked the detective. "Oh, yes," she said, "but I was confused and I didn't notice how much." "You did see it being snatched?" queried the Justice. "Yes," said the woman.

"Then Evelyn went to the other side of the fireplace to the telephone, and he pushed her off the chair and knocked it out of her hand and she knocked her head on the fireplace. Then we gave him our money and he chatted awhile and then he opened the door and told us not to scream, to let him walk out of there, and if we called the guards he said he would come back and burn the house down.

"Before he left he pulled the telephone out of its socket. When we had recovered a little bit, Evelyn went to a gentleman a few doors down and he called the guards."

"I take it you knew the accused before that night," asked the Justice. "Oh, I used to see him knocking around, but we had more to do with his brother, Kevin. I shouldn't have opened the door. I know that."

"But he had asked you for work earlier that day," asked the defence solicitor. "Yes, but it was money he wanted at night," she pointed out.

She agreed that he probably hadn't meant to hurt her sister when he pushed her away from the phone.

The two other witnesses couldn't come because of their medical condition and age, the detective said, concluding his case.

"The best course for my client is to admit the offence as set out," said the defence solicitor, "but if I may, I would like to say a few words about his background, which I learned about this morning."

"I'll pass this down to you, and you can read it," said the Justice, who already had before him a report on the man. The solicitor read it and said, "Well, Justice, if you've read this too, I know you'll take it into account." "Oh, I will, yes," said the Justice.

"There's just one or two other things I want to mention." The solicitor began: "Since he was released from prison he has been unemployed for 12 months. He has spent four terms in St. Brendan's — four months, six weeks, three weeks and one month, respectively. I also found out that at the age of 10½ his schooling was interrupted by rheumatic fever and he spent 10 months in the hospital and another two years and two and a half months in a convalescent home. So, in fact, he left school at 10½, and he was indeed very backward at school. So that I think, in addition to the facts mentioned in the psychiatrist's report, one has to take into account the fact that the man was backward at school and not very intelligent. Ah, um, I think, Justice, I can't say anything more."

The Justice said he would convict the man of constructive burglary and breaking and entering.

The detective said he had not got the man's previous convictions to hand at that moment.

"Excuse me," the man spoke for the first time, "I'd like to point out that I left Mountjoy in August after doing 12 months."

"Well, I've no doubt he terrified the ladies and I sentence him to 12 months to run concurrently on each charge, with a recommendation for suitable medical treatment in Mountjoy," said the Justice. The man said he wanted to appeal. The Justice fixed bail at an independent surety of £200.

18 October 1973

Shrinkage

Anybody could tell you, the C.I.E. worker said, that magazines often came adrift from bundles that were in transit. He had merely taken such a loose magazine, gone into the parcels office to read it, during the slack period, and had every intention of returning it. Then along came the guard.

The magazine, priced at 40p, was about amateur photography. The worker told the defence solicitor that he had never been in trouble before, had a well-paid, trustworthy job with the company, involving rapid promotion, and had once worked for 10 months as a social worker with Shelter Referral. He also had worked at night with the Simon Community.

A second C.I.E. worker went into the dock of Dublin District Court 4 to testify on his own behalf before District Justice Good.

"I started work at 1.45 exactly", he said. "I'm a mails porter. There were some loose magazines on the barrow."

"How do you mean, loose?" asked the Justice.

"The top ones were loose," said the man. "I took one, and started to read it. When I had finished it, I took the *Daily Mirror* out of my pocket, and I was just going to replace the magazine when the guard appeared and asked me for my name and address. Before that he said that if I didn't give it, he would take me down to the station and force it out of me. I'm no thief. I was going to put it back on the barrow."

"Did you fold it up and wrap it in the newspaper?" asked the Justice.

"No. I had it in me hand," said the man.

"The guard says he saw you fold it up and wrap it in a newspaper," said the Justice.

"I took the magazine to read, which I did read it, and I was going to put it back," said the man. "When I was working at another station, sure I found a £10 note and handed it up to the station-master."

"Did you take it and walk away?" asked the defence solicitor.

"No", said the man. "I just moved four feet away."

"Did you put it in your pocket?" asked the Justice.

"I did not," said the man. "I had a hole in me pocket. It wouldn't have gone in."

"You had the *Daily Mirror* in your pocket," pointed out the Justice.

"That was the other pocket," said the man. "This pocket," he pulled out the lining of his jacket, "is torn." So it was.

He told the solicitor he had been in continuous employment for 11 years of which three were spent with C.I.E. He had never been in trouble before. He was 38 years old and married.

"Why did you tell the guard you knew nothing about the magazine when you had it on you?" asked the Justice.

"Because I was confused," said the man.

"What was the reason for your confusion?" asked the Justice.

"Because I am not in the habit of stealing," said the man. "I was on the premises, and I was going to put it back."

"But why not admit you had the magazine in your possession? Didn't you tell a lie by saying you didn't have it?" asked the Justice.

"It was a lie," admitted the man.

"Why didn't you say you just took it to read it and were going to put it back?" asked the Justice.

"I did take it up just to read it," said the man. "But I was confused when he asked me."

"Again I don't understand," said the Justice. "Why were you confused? To me the matter appears to have been simple."

The man was silent.

"Do you deny taking the magazine?" asked the prosecuting inspector.

"I don't deny taking the magazine," said the man.

"The guard says he was 20 feet away and saw you

remove the magazine from the bundle," said the inspector.

"The guard stands against the wall and the wall is 20 feet away," said the man.

"I have to suggest to you that the guard is not chained to the wall and that he can move about," said the inspector.

The Justice recalled the guard.

"You testified that you saw these men remove the magazine from bundles that were tied with twine," said the Justice. "Do you have any doubt as to whether or not the magazines were loose? I mean, if you have any doubt, please help me."

The guard said that the magazines were tied with either twine or wrapper. He had no doubt that both men removed the magazines from intact bundles. He clearly saw the second man wrap his magazine in the *Daily Mirror*.

The defence solicitor said that the matter hung on whether or not both men had the intention of permanently depriving the owner of the magazines. He submitted that they intended to return the magazines. He had a second point to make.

"The consequences to both men, if they are convicted, even if they are only fined, is that they will immediately be sacked."

"I think you should leave the matter of consequences to me," said the Justice.

He summed up.

"From the point of view of the defendants, this is a very serious case, though the articles involved in the larceny charge are of minimal value.

"I must decide whether these men, or either one of them, deliberately stole one magazine each. I must say I was very impressed with the evidence of the guard. He gave his evidence very clearly. He was in no doubt about what he saw, though he was subjected very properly, to a long cross-examination by the defence solicitor. It is very hard for me to accept that these men saw the magazines lying loosely on the top of the bundle and that they took them up just to read them. I don't accept their testimony, I'm sorry to say.

"I accept the guard's evidence that he saw them remove

them from tied-up bundles. How they intended to put them back, I don't know and I'll probably never know ... I cannot, in all conscience, find any doubt in my mind ... there has been very strong evidence from the guard and I accept his evidence without question.

"I will impose a fine of £3 each, with one month to pay and fourteen days in default."

The men appealed.

29 October 1975

A difficult man

"Would you put out that cigarette. How dare you," roared the justice. "Sorry," said the man amiably, neither daring nor defensive, and he moved into the dock, where he sat himself down. His face was large and red and solid, under cropped stiff white hair. His body was big and strong and unbent though he was old. The witness went into the box in Dublin District Court 4 to tell District Justice Ó hUadhaigh his story.

"I am an inspector in Dublin Corporation," he stated precisely. "On the sixth of January last, at 10.40 p.m. approximately, I collected the defendant in my car to place him on a job where he was detailed as a watchman. I did this because he hadn't turned up for his work at 5 p.m. though he had indicated at 3.30 that he would be there at five. He stated in a very aggressive attitude and abusive language that he hadn't been able to find the job he was marked for. I mentioned to him that he could have telephoned, and that I would have got a call on the radio, and come to collect him. He got very aggressive at this and then became silent for a while. As we were turning into a road he let fly with his fist and knocked my spectacles off and broke the frame and cut my lip. The car went off the road and struck another car that was parked at the kerb."

The inspector sat back.

The justice asked the defendant if he wished to cross-examine the witness.

"What about medical — I mean legal aid? Isn't there

151

something about legal aid I can get?" asked the defendant.

"There's such a thing as free legal aid but you can't get it on this charge," said the justice.

"Very good, very good," nodded the man. "Well, there's one question I want to ask the inspector. I've been working with the corporation for three or four years. I'm what you call a watchman, or at least I was. I've put up with a lot in that time, I've been abused, because men like the inspector have no respect. . ."

"That's a statement. Have you any questions you want to ask?" interrupted the justice.

"Well, I had gone in that morning to pack up the job. . .", began the man again.

"Do you want to ask the witness any questions about what he said?" asked the justice, and he summarised the witness's evidence, ending with the blow that had been struck. "I agree with that," nodded the man.

"I'm not asking you to agree. I'm only repeating the evidence," said the justice.

"You were very aggressive to me," the man turned to the witness. "You pushed me about when you came into the hostel."

The inspector denied this. He talked about the difficulty of his job, making sure the watchmen were there, and related worries.

"He shouldn't be in that job at all. He should be out on the road to see what it's like," said the man, with fine contempt.

The justice again asked if he wished to cross-examine.

"When he got into the car he started exaggerating, saying I shouldn't have done this, I would get into trouble over it, what would the big boss say, and I got annoyed," said the man.

The justice invited him to make a statement then, or remain silent.

The man elected for sworn testimony in the witness box. He took the oath, settled himself quietly into the chair, and gazed thoughtfully at the justice. The justice gazed back. There was a philosophic silence. The man folded his hands in his lap and pondered them, peacefully.

"Fire away," the justice broke the mood.

"Ah yes," the man roused himself. "Well, what happened was this, I went in that morning to pack up the job all right. The man there asked me to do one more night and said he'd put it into my pay. So I said I would. The job was five or six miles away, in Marino. It was a terrible wet evening. I went down there to look for the job. I got talking to a man there, and he said: 'There's no job here.' Well, that has happened to me before, you see, and more than once. I've gone there and I wasn't wanted at all. I went back to the hostel and went to bed. The next thing, around nine or 10 at night, somebody's saying 'get up' and I didn't know who it was at all.

"It was him, and he said 'get up quick,' so I did: I hurried myself. Well, we got into the car, and he was nagging, and saying what was going to happen to me, and he went on and on. Well, my patience was exhausted. I put up with a great deal from him, but he went too far this time. 'Sure these things happen,' I said to him. 'It's happened to me. I've gone to a job, and I wasn't needed. It happens.' I've been there nearly six years, justice, and I've put up with a lot. The watchman gets stones pegged at him, he gets abused, and these inspectors here don't think about that. Once my radio was stolen. Stones pegged at me. Abuse."

The man mused quietly. Then he resumed his tale. "I don't deny I hit him. But if he hadn't said anything, had just stopped nagging, it wouldn't have happened. He annoyed me. These things happen to everybody, but he wouldn't stop talking about it. Haven't I been let down at work myself? Anyway, I've never hit a man before, never been in trouble before, never been in court before. That's nearly all I have to say now, justice. That's the whole truth."

"No questions," said the prosecuting guard.

"If he had played fair with me, I would have played fair with him," added the man. "But there's a limit to any man's endurance, and he pushed me past mine. It was a terrible night, too. So what do you think yourself now, justice? What's your opinion? I've given you mine."

"Are you saying all the truth? I saw you smiling very quietly when the guard spoke just now," said the justice.

The man smiled again to himself. "Well, there is one thing, I suppose," he said. "The guards came up to the hostel to give me the summons. They started kicking down the door of the room I was sleeping in, I thought the place was on fire. I don't know how you'd feel about it, justice, if they came in the middle of the night and started kicking down your door to summons you. Isn't the day long enough for that?"

"I wouldn't like to be summoned night or day," said the justice.

"But if you have to, the day's long enough for it," said the man. "And there they were, in the middle of the night, kicking down my bedroom door."

"Your bedroom?" emphasised the justice sardonically.

"Yes, my bedroom" said the man, ignoring the slight on his place of abode.

"What did you do before you were a night watchman?" asked the justice, his curiosity aroused, his tone not rough.

"I was in England for a time at the factory work," said the man, who was not awe-struck. "And I was at the building. Then I worked here in Dublin. And I did some farm work. I used to cut turf in the bogs for Bord na Mona. Then I worked at the watchman for five or six years, but I had to put up with a lot there."

He was "about 60," he answered the justice, who was showing signs of fascination.

Another silence.

"I'll have to convict you. You struck him and you admitted it", said the justice.

"I hit him all right", agreed the man, as though they were discussing simple arithmetic.

"I don't want to sentence you to jail. I'll make it six months' imprisonment, suspended for six months. There's no point fining you, because you haven't any money, isn't that right?" asked the justice.

"Well, I have a bit of money", said the man.

"Have you money in a Post Office book?" asked the

justice.

"Yes, but I could be doing with it, instead of spending it on a fine", said the man, sensibly.

"I'd say you have a fair bit salted away, and you working all your life", said the justice cannily.

"I don't know about that" said the man. "But I haven't left it all in the pubs anyway".

"I'd say you're a difficult man", observed the justice, putting distance between them, now that it was time to judge. "I know the type of man you are, particularly coming from the part of the country you come from. You can't go around hitting people you know".

The man had no previous convictions, said the guard.

"I forgot about the damage. What about the inspector's glasses?" asked the justice. "What do you have to say about that?".

Damage amounted to £35, said the guard.

"I don't know about the glasses", the man said. "If he hadn't annoyed me, you see—".

"You're pushing things too far", snapped the justice. "You've gotten away with murder so far. You're getting off very lightly".

"I get free spectacles myself, from the insurance card", said the man.

"I'll bet you get a lot of things free", said the justice. "But the inspector's not entitled to that, with the job he's got. Now are you making me an offer about the spectacles?"

"I don't know", said the man, "I just don't know".

"You've gone very quiet now", said the justice triumphantly.

"I can't afford it", said the man stubbornly.

"You have money saved", said the justice.

"I'll want that to live on. I won't always be working. I'll maybe need it when I'm unemployed", said the man.

"You've got a fair bit coming to you on the dole", said the justice.

"I've no English cards", said the man. "And you can't draw the dole after six months".

"The spectacles cost £3 to repair", said the inspector, from the public benches.

"Ah, now", said the man, brightening.

"Well, now what do you say?" asked the justice.

"I could pay that, but I'd need an hour or two, or I could bring it tomorrow", said the man.

"Are you married or single?" the justice asked, curiosity still whetted.

"Single", said the man.

"I'll remand you till Thursday. Bring the money then", said the justice. "And don't get into any more trouble".

"Oh you won't see me here any more", said the man.

"I'm sure I won't", the justice paid his awkward tribute.

14 January 1975

A stolen car

Huckleberry Finn appeared in Dublin Court 6, yesterday, before District Justice Good. His father and mother came up from the farm in Kerry to hear the saga, which began one Sunday night, when, the father said, "he went out to the dance or the pictures, and then strolled off. I didn't hear from him again until the guards came a month later and told us".

It was a complicated case, the prosecuting guard told the Justice, and he settled back in the witness box. Huckleberry's co-defendant would not be appearing as he was now unfortunately detained in a mental institution down the country. The charge involved a car, which was stolen originally from Bangor, Co. Down, Northern Ireland. The number plates had been switched in the South, and the accused was eventually found in possession of the car, though he had not taken it in the first instance.

Huckleberry, who pleaded guilty, went into the witness box to tell his tale. He was small, bespectacled, neatly dressed and nineteen. "I met another fellow", he said, "and we thumbed to Dublin. We couldn't get a job, and we stayed in the hostel. I met this crowd who were working for a man, putting down tarmacadam, and me and the fellow went to work with them.

"I thought we would be living in houses, but we were living in caravans. It was all right for the first two or three

156

nights, but when we got away from Dublin he started paying us 50p a day instead of £3 a day we were supposed to get. So we kept going with them for about three weeks, working down the roads until we got to Waterford. We were still only getting 50p a day.

"So we decided we'd take his car. It was the only transport we could get. It was parked outside the pub. I drove it as far as Kilkenny, and my friend drove it on to another village from there. That night we slept in the car. The next day my friend drove it to Dublin, and we put it into a car park. We waited around Dublin for a few days. We used to get food in the hostels. We slept in the car in the car park. The guards pulled in beside us and we got caught".

His father said that the son was a "wonderful boy", and they had a happy home. His son had now returned home and was helping him again on the farm. That meant he had two sons at home working with him.

"Answer me this simple, straightforward question", the Justice leaned towards Huckleberry. "Why did you do it?" We waited with bated breath. "I don't know", said Huckleberry.

"But you have a very decent father", said the amazed Justice, "and you have a very happy home. Is there any reason why you would suddenly leave home? You were very well brought up, apparently". Huckleberry looked at him steadfastly. "Do you appreciate now that it was a very stupid thing to do?", the Justice rattled on. "Aren't you happy at home? Do you intend staying at home now with your father?" Huckleberry looked at him.

"I think we can take it that this isn't going to happen again, can't we?", Huckleberry's solicitor urged on him. Huckleberry nodded. "You knew, of course, that you were driving an uninsured car? Did you have a driving licence? Did you ever drive before?", the Justice came in.

He had driven before and he had a provisional driving licence, said Huckleberry. "Can we take it also that, if you considered you had been paid proper wages, you wouldn't have taken the car?", asked the solicitor. Huckleberry nodded.

"There's very little I can add, Justice", said the solicitor. "I must ask you to be as lenient as you can under the circumstances. I would implore you not to send him to prison. He co-operated fully with the guards, he comes from an excellent family, and he's never been in trouble before".

The Justice convicted. He would take into account the solicitor's very eloquent plea urging leniency, he said, and the fact of co-operation with the guards, who had said they believed Huckleberry's story to be 100% true, and the fact that his father was a decent, hard-working man, and the fact that Huckleberry himself appeared to be a very decent boy. "But", he continued, "I cannot understand why an 18½ years old boy would want to leave home, seeking adventure elsewhere". He was worried that Huckleberry had not stopped to consider how his parents would feel, "having a son there one day and not there the next". But, all things considered, and though he usually jailed men for stealing cars, he said, he would impose a three-month suspended prison sentence.

"Now leave", the Justice smiled. "Go back home with your parents. Let me not see you here again".

And Huckleberry left the Dublin court and went back down to the farm in the country with his mother and father.

16 May 1974

Men of standing

After meeting Mr. Black with his two front teeth in his hand, and his mouth bleeding, he had gone to the night-club and arrested Mr. White, the guard told District Justice Good in Dublin District Court 6.

Mr. Black took the stand. He was dressed in a non-descript grey suit, with a striped tie and a cardigan. His eyes were soft and brown, his hair waved just a little over the collar of his shirt.

In the dock sat Mr. White. He wore a close-fitting three-piece pin-striped suit, with a thick gold chain across the breast. His hair was short and tight against his head, his eyes sharp blue.

Mr. Black's barrister had requested that the case finish after the morning's adjournment, because his client was due to go abroad on the morrow.

"It appears", said the Justice to Mr. Black, "that there was some litigation between you and Mr. White. There had been proceedings in the High Court that day".

"Yes", said Mr. Black. "Mr. White took an action against me for breach of partnership. The case was fought, and we won, with costs. I adjourned to the bar of the Four Courts, where I had an orange. I don't drink too much. I was with my solicitor, and we met two leading members of the Bar there, and we went on to Dublin's leading Watering Spot for lunch, where we had two bottles of wine. Then the four of us went for a drive into Wicklow, where we had tea at a well-known place. After that we returned to the Watering Spot. I had not seen Mr. White since the case finished that morning.

"He was in the Watering Spot and he shouted across to my table: 'There is Black, the lying, perjuring bastard. You bought off Judge X ——. X —— is a lying hack. He is your puppet. I'll go to jail before I pay costs.' We left the Watering Spot, despite the fact that we had ordered fresh drinks, and went off to Dublin's Latest Night Club for a meal. I am ignorant of the place, myself, Justice — but we went there with the two leading members of the Bar. They stayed with us. My solicitor, as you know Justice, is very amusing company. In the night club, we had one bottle of wine and a great talk, and we danced. One of the Bar members has a great interest in classical music — "

"Who are you trying to impress?", broke in Mr. White's solicitor.

"Mr. White then entered the night club", continued Mr. Black, unperturbed, "and said the same things that he had said two hours earlier, except that he added, to one of my lady guests, 'You're the perjurer's bitch', but that's only a minor detail".

Mr. Black's solicitor had told him that Mr. White was possibly acting in contempt, and the solicitor approached

Mr. White to warn him of this. Mr. Black went off to get his party's coats.

At that stage they were grouped in the night club "around a sort of pool, about 10 feet by five . . . no, it's not a swimming pool, Justice, but they have women dancing around in it, very scantily-dressed ladies".

"Women dancing in the swimming pool?", asked the surprised Justice.

"Staff only, not the guests", smiled Mr. Black. "Anyway, Mr. White spoke to the owner of the night club and —"

He produced three photographs from a file. They were colour pictures of his gaping mouth, showing lips drawn back from upper and lower teeth. There was a gap in the upper set of molars. The pictures were reminiscent of the stills from "Jaws".

"I'm objecting to these photographs", said Mr. White's solicitor, stretching across Mr. Black's barrister and slapping the photographs face down onto the witness stand. Mr. Black held them up again. Mr. White's solicitor pushed them down.

"I'm in charge of this case. Please keep yourself under control", the Justice rebuked the solicitor.

Mr. White had struck him, continued Mr. Black, "and my natural teeth broke and fell into my hand. He then tried to knee me. I turned around to avoid this blow; luckily I was sober, for if I had been drunk I would have been too slow. I had my hand in my pocket, and his knee broke my key ring and my finger nail". He held up his thumb.

The next morning the manager of the Watering Spot "managed to get me one of the better dentists in Dublin. He's the top dentist, actually, Justice, and the manager got him to cancel all his appointments for that day, and I spent the whole day with him".

"They don't look too bad on you", the Justice smiled.

"But they're not my natural teeth. You can see the difference in colour", Mr. Black smiled back, revealing his two new front teeth. "And may I just add one or two things, Justice . . . four days later I was eating in an inexpensive restaurant in Grafton Street". He named the latest restaurant.

"I wouldn't know the expensive restaurants", smiled the Justice.

"It was an inexpensive restaurant", Mr. Black enunciated clearly, "and my car was parked in a street opposite to the window of the restaurant. I looked out and saw someone who appeared to be interfering with my car. I thought it was being stolen, and I raced out. I was groggy after my session with the top dentist, and I stopped near my car and shouted, 'Mr. White', for it was he, 'this is ridiculous. You must not interfere with my car'. Then I ran back — yes, away from the scene, Justice, — hoping to get a guard. He ran after me, caught up with me at the jeweller's, repeated his remarks concerning the Judge and me, and took a swipe at me, to use the expression. I moved aside and he hit the shutters, but as a result my two new dentures loosened, and I had to get them fixed by my own dentist in the country."

He had not on that occasion, or indeed any other, used language towards Mr. White which was calculated to lead to a breach of the peace. The expenses for the Dublin dentist were £500 and £42 for the country dentist.

Mr. White's solicitor rose to cross-examine. Had Mr. Black been 'victorious' after winning High Court litigation?

"No", said Mr. Black. "We won, but in fact we lost, because we knew Mr. White to be a man of straw, and that we wouldn't get our costs back".

"A man of straw? He has a number of businesses in Dublin", protested the solicitor.

"Call them what you like", sniffed Mr. Black.

"Do you mean he's not as rich as you?", asked the solicitor. Mr. Black ignored the remark.

"Then you went out celebrating with your solicitor and some friends?", pressed Mr. White's solicitor.

"You don't celebrate when you lose money", said Mr. Black.

"Had there been trouble about a cheque in the night-club?" asked the solicitor.

"I tried to offer them a cheque but they refused, which

was understandable, since I'd never been there before", said Mr. Black.

"Do you remember saying anything to the effect that 'In this country money can buy anything?' ", asked the solicitor.

"You're referring to Judge X —— there", said Mr. Black. "It was alleged that I had bought him off. I can assure you that I didn't, of course."

Why had he gone back into the night-club, after leaving consequent on Mr. White's arrival there? asked the solicitor.

"We went in to get witnesses about his behaviour", said Mr. Black.

Mr. White took the stand.

"After the High Court judgement", he said, "I went to my place of business. Then I went into town and met friends in a well-known bar. I was quite shattered by what had happened in court . . . we went on to the Watering Place about nine in the evening. Mr. Black's party was on the left. We were sitting on the right. Mr. Black's solicitor came over to me — we were good friends — and extended his hand to me, and said there had to be a winner and a loser, and that there was no need for us to fall out.

"Unfortunately, some people in my party made remarks that provoked me, and I made remarks to Mr. Black's solicitor that I regret. Someone in my company made a remark to the effect that you can't beat the old party, and the solicitor and I had more or less believed in the same things . . . I certainly lost my head, but not about the judge. I certainly called Mr. Black a lying, perjuring bastard . . . anything I called him I believe he richly deserved, and I don't regret those remarks. I think he perjured, not alone in the High Court, but in this court as well . . . he passed a comment about his wealth and money, which he seems to rely on for everything. He said 'Money talks. You shouldn't have bothered' . . . Later, in the night-club, he put his foot out as I was passing by, and I turned round. You could say, I suppose, that I struck him. I pushed him, with my closed hand. His solicitor said to me, 'Cool it, this is getting out of hand'. He and I could have settled the matter without personalities getting involved. I accept the version that his solicitor gave in this morning's evidence. I accept that he gave it in all sincerity and truth . . . I struck Mr. Black then in the face . . . I told the night-club owner that I was sorry this had happened in his club, but that I wasn't sorry I had hit Mr. Black. I told him I thought I had been set up".

Four days later Mr. Black had accused him of interfering with Mr. Black's car, and Mr. White had called the doorman of the well-known restaurant to witness that he wasn't near Mr. Black's car. But Mr. Black had said, "I'll have you again now".

Mr. White had asked the doorman to take note of the incident, telling him, "Mr. Black is a dangerous man. I know what he can do in court". But he did not threaten Mr. Black.

Mr. Black's barrister reminded him that, in the High Court, the judge had taken five minutes to dismiss Mr. White's case, with the remark that he couldn't understand why it had been brought in the first place.

He had lost the case on a point of law, Mr. White said, but he had brought it to court on a matter of principle. "I wanted only a farthing's damages, but I realise now that requesting such an amount is in fact disadvantageous."

Returning to the scene of the night-club, Mr. White said that Mr. Black had gone to the exit when he arrived, and then returned to the pool, where he attempted to trip Mr. White.

The barrister pointed out that Mr. Black had merely gone to the cloakroom to get his party's coats. Mr. White argued that it was not reasonable to go to the cloakroom near the exit for coats and then come all the way back into the club with them.

"Have you never heard of a host going to get the coats for his party?", asked the barrister. "Does that not happen in your circle of acquaintance?".

"It doesn't happen in that night club", said Mr. White

stiffly.

Mr. White called a hostess from the night-club to give evidence.

When she had asked Mr. Black to pay for the wine he had ordered, she testified, Mr. Black offered a cheque, saying, "I can't produce a banker's card. You should know me". He was agitated that she didn't know who he was, she said. Later, he had written his foreign business address on the back of a cheque drawn from a bank in the Irish countryside. Later still there had been a fracas in the club, involving Mr. Black and Mr. White, and she had heard the comment "Money talks", though she didn't know who had passed it. Mr. Black was suffering from a nose-bleed, and she had offered him ice in a cloth, "but he wouldn't let me apply it to his nose. He stood there, making an exhibition of himself".

The doorman of the well-known bar testified. He was really the cleaner, he said, but he did duty as doorman on Friday and Saturday nights. Mr. Black had approached him, asking him if he had seen Mr. White interfere with his car. Mr. White had his own car, and would hardly need to steal anyone else's, the doorman had replied. Mr. Black had asked him if he had seen Mr. White commit an assault upon him.

"I said to Mr. Black", the doorman told the Justice, "that if by assault he meant two fellows shouting at each other, without exchanging blows, then they should both be locked up in jail. Mr. Black wanted to get the police. I said to him, 'The guards have more to do in this day and age than look after two eejits like you' ".

"Those are the most sensible words I've heard in this case", said the Justice. "This is a very unfortunate business", he summed up, "emanating from the High Court result that first day. One can understand anybody feeling aggrieved and disappointed when a verdict goes against them . . . it's unfortunate that it should have ended with this bad result . . . assault occasioning actual bodily harm. Mr. White probably regrets it now . . . he is a man of unblemished record. Under normal circumstances, I would impose a custodial sentence, but there is a different atmosphere about this case . . . convict Mr. White, fined £50, two months to pay, or one month's imprisonment in default".

He dismissed charges against both arising out of the incident involving the car.

"These are the type of men we don't like to see in a court of justice", he continued. "They are men of responsibility. Men of standing in the community."

25 March 1976

House Rules

"I am British," the witness said, "or rather Jamaican, to be precise. I am a bricklayer by occupation. I don't know how to address you. Shall I say 'sir?' " "It doesn't matter," replied District Justice Good, in Dublin District Court No. 4.

"I had friends round to visit me," the man said, "a man, his wife and child. She hung my clothes out on the line in the yard, and I went out to the shop, and when I came back she said my washing was on the ground. I said 'Great Scott, I must go and put it back up'. I had my slippers on. There are five steps leading down to the yard, and I stumbled and inadvertently struck with my arm, or some part of my body, the wall of the defendant's room, which is very flimsy. Before I could get outside he came out and struck me a blow on the jaw which knocked me across the passage, skinning my arm, and giving me a bruise on my forehead which is still there. Did I provoke him? Oh, there was no provocation whatsoever, sir.

"Incidentally, sir, I called my friend to my assistance, as I did not intend to retaliate, because I am not so young. I'm over 70. My birthday is on Hallow'een, actually, and he is a young man, about 40–45, and he is bigger and stronger than me. In any case I did not wish to lower myself to public brawling. My friend stood between us, because I had received four or five blows to my head. I'm tough, I know, but I returned to my room. After a few moments the defendant came to my room and banged

165

on my door, and the lady who was there opened it and he came in cursing and blinding, left, right and centre, and he called me . . . do you want to hear what he called me, sir, shall I tell this court what he called me? He called me a dirty black dago bastard in front of my friends, who are really good friends of mine for three years.

"When I first knew them, I struck a really bad patch, and they helped me, and I visited them every night for two years. They visit me now, and anything I can do for them I do. They struck a bad patch and I helped them. I am not a young man and I have no friends in this country . . . the first time I met the defendant was when I went and applied for the room, only the day before I took up residence. Previous to this incident, sir, the defendant was extremely nice to me, and I to him.

"I don't know if I can say this, and you must correct me sir if I can't, but if he came home sometimes intoxicated I would let him come into my room until he became peaceful. I am peaceful, I have been a man of peace all my life. I don't know why he should have turned against me, I gave him no offence whatsoever."

The defence barrister rose to his feet. He placed one shoe on the bench and held onto his robes. "Does my client, who is the caretaker of the house, attempt to collect your rent every week?", was his opening shot. "I beg your pardon," replied the witness, "he does not attempt, he actually collects it."

"Do you know that it is the rule not to hang the washing out on the line,", the barrister thundered, "on Saturdays and Sundays?" "On Sundays," the witness corrected him. "The rule is very clear," said the barrister. "It's not a written rule, it's verbal . . . ," began the witness. "Are you aware of the rule?", said the barrister. "It is verbal," said the witness. "I asked if you were aware of the rule. Please confine yourself to the answer," directed the barrister. The witness answered that he was. "Thank you," said the barrister heavily, "thank you very much. My client's story will be that you banged on his door on a number of occasions."

"That is a complete fabrication," said the witness.

"That is his story," said the barrister. "He can say what he likes," sniffed the old man.

"And did you tell him on a number of occasions," asked the barrister, "that you had a black belt in judo? You never told him that? I wonder why he should say so. Now, it is a very narrow passage, about that wide, is it not?", asked the barrister, widening his hands. "Perhaps I can help you to be more precise, as I am a bricklayer," said the old man. "It is three feet, six inches wide."

"Thank you for your assistance, you've been very helpful," said the barrister. "Now I must put it to you that your story is a complete fabrication, and you had your mind made up to tell it here to strengthen your story." "Let me answer it this way," said the man, "I have a witness here to corroborate it."

The barrister sat down.

The man's friend, also foreign, corroborated the story, saying that he had seen the defendant "beating up" the old man.

"Where did the blow connect?", asked the barrister, and the man said it had connected on the chin. He had only seen one blow struck, he said. "You used the term beating up. What did you mean?", asked the barrister.

"I mean," said this man, "that I saw somebody up against the wall getting a punch."

The barrister sat down.

The defendant said that he was the caretaker of the house, which his father owned, and his job was to keep the house in order by doing little jobs. "The Drug Squad found drugs in the house last December, and they had to keep it under observation. My job is to keep the house in order . . . I believe that if anybody has to do washing, five days a week is sufficient. On Saturday night I myself don't want to look out and see dirty underwear hanging there. It's a gross insult. When I went to collect this man's rent on Friday night he told me I could bloody well wait until he was bloody well ready. I had to take this abuse. On Saturday night I came in and saw this underwear, socks and all, so I disconnected the line, and it dropped on the grass.

"It was a beautiful sunny day. When he came down I was pretty scared because he told me he was a colonel in the British Army, and had a judo belt and was interested in wrestling, and could break a block with his hand. Even if he is old, he could have one leg and a karate belt and still knock a man down. He gave a demanding knock on my door and I got nervous, and he asked if I had let down the line. I told him he knew the rules. He swung at me, and I said to myself I might lose, but I might as well defend myself, and I gave him one little slap. He talks about a bruise, but I don't see any in court.

"I didn't go up to his room then, I went up later. I saw his door open, and he had a woman there and a friend I don't know, but he should have had the door closed and not be letting the whole house know about it. His friend challenged me, and it was me that rang the guards."

The Justice asked him why he had not just asked the man to remove the clothes from the line.

"Well", he said, "he had put them out the previous Friday night, saying Saturday begins at one o'clock, and he had just done it to provoke me. He never uses that line."

The Justice said the defendant seemed to be a decent man, but he had lost his temper and shouldn't have. The barrister said he was a nervous person and an ex-soldier.

The Justice fined him £5 for assault.

25 July 1973

Considering the evidence

"I'm not guilty, your honour, because I was . . ." the man said from the dock of the Dublin District Court. The District Justice interrupted swiftly. "I don't care why you aren't guilty. That's not my concern at the moment.

"Are you ready to go on with the case today? You are? Guard, what is the amount of the damage? You don't know yet? You'll have to prove it during the case."

The guard said that the damage — to a two-foot square window in a new bus — was under £50.

He said that as a result of a radio call, he went to where the bus was parked on its route.

"There was a certain amount of fuss going on . . . and a window on the bus had been broken. As a result of what I was told, I arrested the defendant who was walking away down the road."

The bus conductor told the court: "Well, first of all, this man here," he pointed to the defendant, "boarded the bus along with another man. Then this man here took out the fare . . . yes, Justice, I approached him . . . and he took out his fare and then he got up and caught me by the throat.

"His pal and the driver of the bus held him back when he made a kick at me. Then he put his foot through the window . . ."

The conductor added: "So he got off the bus then and they picked him up further down the road. The driver of the bus went along in the squad car and identified him."

The guard asked whether much disturbance was caused. "Ah, not very much," said the conductor. "The passengers were transferred to another bus and nobody was injured."

The District Justice asked the defendant if he wished to cross-examine the witness. "Your honour," he said. "I can't remember anything about what he says."

"You're denying it in other words," said the District Justice. "I'm not", said the man. "I take tablets, you see. Can I explain it to you?".

"You can do it like goodo, as they say, afterwards," said the District Justice. "But first do you want to cross-examine?" The man shook his head.

The bus driver was called. "When we got as far as Christ Church this man caused a commotion," he said. "I noticed that my conductor was in trouble, so I called the radio controller who called the guards.

"I then went to the assistance of my conductor. This man had apparently caught him — yes, Justice, I saw him catching hold of the conductor — and his friend that accompanied him restrained him.

"My conductor retreated to the rear of the bus and I stood in the centre of the passageway. He made a couple of kicks past me at my conductor and then he made for the front of the bus.

"He turned round, caught the passenger rail and swung his feet up and through the window. The gardai arrived and caught him up the road."

The defendant declined to cross-examine him.

The guard said: "There's supposed to be a witness here from the maintenance section of C.I.E." There was no witness around so he closed his case.

"The witness is not here to give evidence as to the amount of damage caused," said the District Justice, "so the defendant is entitled to a dismissal of charge two relating to the window."

"Now, then, mister, what do you want to do about this?" And the District Justice turned his head and addressed himself to the wall as he reeled off quickly the choices open to the defendant, about speaking or not speaking, speaking from the dock as opposed to an oath and about speaking on oath leaving him liable to cross-examination.

Then the District Justice turned his gaze from the wall to the defendant in the dock, and awaited his choice of action.

"I take these tablets, you see", said the man. "I met this chap, I knew him long ago, and we had a drink together. Then this incident happened and I don't know if I'm guilty or not guilty. I must say, if I have done it, I'm very sorry about it". He trailed into silence. "I'm an epileptic", he added.

The District Justice uttered one word. "Convict."

"The defendant has one previous conviction," said the guard. "You say you're an epileptic," said the District Justice. "Where were you drinking? Does drinking affect the effect of the tablets? Where's your doctor to prove that? Where's the proof that you're an epileptic? Epileptics don't swing on railings or bars. I thought epileptics fell into fits on the ground. But the driver says you put your two hands around the railing and swung into the air and put your feet through the window."

"I don't remember," said the man.

"Are you suggesting you were in the process of having a fit?", asked the District Justice.

"Oh, no, I don't say that," said the man. "It's just that I had been taking tablets."

"Were you in a fit?," asked the District Justice. "I wasn't, no," said the man.

"Well, what's your excuse then?," asked the District Justice. "You can't come in here and say you did it because of drink and expect that to be the end of it. You took the drink of your own volition."

"The maintenance man is here," said the guard.

"Too late," said the District Justice. "You can't mend your hand now. He got a dismissal on that charge. I'm convicting on charges two and three.

"Well, you may be an epileptic. But you're just telling me that as a bald fact. You weren't in the process of a fit when this happened. You suggest you're not supposed to take drink when you take pills. But you did and you must suffer the consequences. Do you work? What's your occupation?"

"I'm a barman, but I'm not working at the moment," he said.

"Why not? There's no shortage of work in that line," said the District Justice.

"I haven't been all that well and I had to stop," said the man. "Well, I don't know about that," said the District Justice. "But it's too late now to be sorry. You put your feet through the window and though that charge is dropped, I'm entitled to take the fact into consideration. You're a man of previous good character, and you're epileptic, but you assaulted the bus conductor, an inoffensive man. One month's imprisonment for the assault and £2 fine for disorderly conduct."

"Your honour, your honour," called a woman from the back of the court. "I'm his sister and he takes fits". She was on her feet and coming forward.

The District Justice was snapping his fingers at the court guard. "Put her out," he said.

"He takes fits very badly and if he's put away for a month in jail he'll take worse fits," said the woman, still approaching and in dire agitation. The guard intercepted her and put her out the door. You could hear her explaining to the guard, that her brother was an epileptic.

The District Justice was already talking to a solicitor on the bench below him. "Why are you talking to an accused man in the dock?," he asked the solicitor furiously. "He mentioned an appeal and I was telling him to speak up," said the solicitor in embarrassment.

But a second sister was on her feet at the back of the court. "I'm his sister too, your honour," she called out tearfully. "He takes pheno-barbitone. When it mixes with drink it does things to his mind."

The District Justice snapped his fingers at her. "Out of this court. I'm well aware of the tablets. Out. You there go down," he pointed to the man in the dock who turned and went down the stairs to the cells while his sister went out the door, both of them meekly going their separate ways.

1 March 1975

The quality of mercy

"He made his mark on the statement because he's not able to read or write", the guard told District Justice Good in Dublin District Court. "He's 21 years old and married with two children."

In the dock sat the defendant, a mild-looking man dressed in his best cheap clothes. He had been caught in the act of breaking into a clothing firm, convicted and given a suspended sentence. Fingerprints taken had shown that he had broken into the same firm the week before, for which offence he was now charged. He had at that time taken some clothes, valued at £44, which he claimed to have subsequently sold in a pub to a stranger.

"Do you know anything about him?" the Justice asked the guard.

"I don't," said the guard. "I only came across him on this occasion. I hadn't known him before. Perhaps his solicitor could help." The solicitor rose to his feet.

"This man and his wife and two young children are living in a flat for which they pay £5.20 a week rent", he said. "The only explanation offered by him to me for the commission of this offence is that he was under severe financial strain at the time. He was in receipt of ten pounds a week unemployment benefit, having stopped work because he had received a bang on the face and was attending hospital.

"He's the sixth eldest of a family of 16 children, Justice. He was 15 when his mother died, and his father left the housing estate where they lived to return to the city centre area to live, taking some of the children with him. From that period on, my client lived in hostels in Dublin and England, where he worked as a labourer.

"Shortly after they were married and living in Yorkshire, their first child got sick and his wife was worried about it, so they decided to return to Dublin. He works at mending lawnmowers, going round houses and knocking on doors. On days when he gets work he can earn up to five or six pounds a day".

The Justice wanted to know why the man had broken into the same premises twice.

"I presume he went back the second time because he hadn't been caught the first time", said the solicitor. He said that the man was obviously inexperienced in crime since he hadn't even worn gloves to avoid fingerprints.

"And he went in by the same window as the first one he had broken", said the guard. "You wouldn't believe the size of it. It was very small. I don't think a child could have gotten in that way".

"He's very slim," commented the Justice. He went on to wonder why the man had done these deeds.

"I'd say he was a victim of circumstances. He had no money", said the guard, sympathetically.

The Justice went on to worry about his claim to have sold the goods in pubs. "It's an old, old story", he said. "It's so old I'm getting sick and tired of it".

"Strangely enough I believe him" said the guard. "I know the particular pub where he went."

"Well, Mister Solicitor," said the Justice, "what do you want of me as regards this man?"

"Well, Justice", said the solicitor, "it's not as though he had a long previous record. And he did co-operate with the guards. He's met the case fairly at any rate. Given his background — his family broken up at an early age, and faring for himself by living in hostels — he has endeavoured to provide for his wife and children."

"He couldn't even sign the marriage register", the Justice snorted.

"That may not have been entirely his fault, given the conditions under which he was reared", said the solicitor delicately.

"Oh, I know, I've met many cases of people unable to read or write" said the Justice. "It's difficult to explain."

"Well, his mother did die while he was young and he had to fend for himself", said the solicitor. His wife was in court, he added.

"I'm placed in a dilemma", said the Justice. "There's obviously no chance of recovering the goods and, given this man's financial background, he won't be able to pay compensation. There's no use fooling ourselves".

"He lives in bad circumstances", said the guard, referring to the defendant's dilemma, as opposed to the clothing firm's.

"And he has no regular occupation to follow", said the Justice. "What does he propose to do, assuming I give him a chance?"

"He proposes to continue mending lawn mowers", said the solicitor. "Perhaps a Probation Officer could help him?"

The Justice said he was only too happy to put him in the care of a Probation Officer. "Four people living on that amount of money", the Justice commented wonderingly.

"It's only seven pounds a week after the rent has been paid", said the solicitor.

"I don't know how any one could rear a family on that", said the Justice. "Pay rent, feed and clothe themselves on this paltry sum. It's astonishing how they manage to exist. The only problem is where this leads to the commission of crime. And that's not going to solve the problem."

"I think he knows that now", said the solicitor.

The Justice decided to impose a six-month suspended sentence and place the man under the care of a Probation Officer. "I take it his home life is a happy one?" he asked.

"Oh it is, Justice. There's no trouble in that line", said the guard.

"I'm glad to hear that", said the Justice. "Well, now, Mr. Murphy, the guard has not said anything against you. If anything, he has spoken in your favour, and the solicitor has spoken up for you, and now you have the benefit of a Probation Officer. What more could we do for you?"

5 March 1975

No time to lose

It was late afternoon before their case was called. Two young girls and two young boys from a built-up housing area came up from the cells and appeared in the dock of Dublin District Court 6 before District Justice Good. A youthful prosecuting guard took the witness stand.

"I was on patrol duty yesterday evening (Sunday)," he said. "I went into the schoolyard and found the four defendants there. When questioned — they were in a shed in the rear of the schoolyard, justice, an open bicycle shed — they would give no reason for being there. They can get over the wall into the yard, justice, it's not a high wall, but in fact last night the gate was open — it was between nine and 10 o'clock."

The justice asked the tallest boy what he was doing in the schoolyard.

"We were standing in the shed, talking," he said languidly.

"Standing in the shed, talking," repeated the justice.

"The shed is in the open," continued the boy. "It's out right in the middle of the yard."

"No, justice," intervened the guard. "It's at the rear of the school."

"It's right in front of the school, facing the road," said the boy, perplexed. His companions nodded their heads. "And we were just standing there," he said again.

"You were just standing in a shed," said the justice.

"They had wine in their possession," the guard came in.

"You had wine in your possession," the justice accused them.

"We were drinking. The girls weren't," said the boy, smiling.

"The girls weren't," the justice repeated in a different tone. He pondered their youthful faces. "I don't see how they could have been up to any mischief, with all due respect, guard," he concluded.

"Well, windows have been broken in the school at certain times," said the guard. "Also," he added, "when they were charged, Smith gave a false name."

"Why did you do that?" the justice asked Smith.

"I don't know. It just came out of me," said Smith. "My right name was on my club card," and he produced his club card.

"Do you always come out with the wrong name? Are you afraid of anything?" the justice asked. The boy did not reply. "Well, guard," the justice resumed, "I don't think that . . . will you keep away from the schoolyard? Will you do your drinking in another place? You'd no right to be there. Alright, then, I'm dismissing the charge."

The four young people, who had been in a school bicycle shed at nine o'clock on a cold Sunday night, left the court.

They had been in custody from Sunday night at 10 o'clock until four o'clock on Monday afternoon. They were kept first in a police station, overnight, and then in the Bridewell underground cells during the morning and afternoon.

All of them were in employment, and all of them had lost a day's work. They did not fancy telling their employers the reason for their absence, they told me afterwards. It wouldn't look good. They told me they had been refused station bail, and that they had asked for their parents to be contacted. They were sure their parents had not been told. I went to the guard and spoke to him.

Had the parents of the young people been contacted, as requested?

He did not know, he said. He had gone off duty.

Why were they not given station bail?

He did not know.

Why were they held so long in custody?

"One of them gave the wrong name," he said. "We had to check out their real names."

"By contacting their parents?" I asked.

No, he said, they had identification on them.

Why were they held all night, after identification had been established?

"They had to be identified, and then questioned and then charged," he said. "It takes a long time."

Did it require all night? I asked.

The guard walked away. What was the name of the station sergeant where they had been held, I asked.

"I haven't got time to be talking to you," he said.

18 November 1975

An intolerable situation

The solicitor put the woman in the witness box of Dublin District Court 4, and baldly asked her one question. "Will you ask the justice to give your son a chance?"

Her son had just been convicted, along with two others, of robbery with violence. They had attacked a man in a side alley. The son looked different from his companions, the way people do who wear suits in a world of jeans.

The woman sat, in a sudden focus, the personal element in a legal line of arrest, prosecution, conviction and impending punishment. Between conviction and punishment she obtruded, raw and intimate, and we watched her suspend the process. Her son receded into the background.

"Well, justice, I beg you to give him a chance," she said. She begged and was not ashamed of the word.

"He is my son," she went on, relentlessly. "He has never given any trouble to me. He has been out of work for six months now, and I could see him get into bad company. I know he's bad with his nerves, justice, because when he's watching T.V. he keeps changing over from one film to another. He can't even stay still when he eats. He won't sit down for long enough. Those two called for him that night and he went out with them . . . he was attending the doctor with an ulster . . .

"I had five children, justice, and I lost two boys. He's the only son I had," she rushed to a halt. The only son she had, the final clincher in her plea.

District Justice Ó hUadhaigh replied quickly.

"One son is the same as one daughter. That's an Irish myth."

"The two girls are married," she bolstered her stand.

"Right," said the justice straightening up.

"But I beg of you, justice, to give him a chance," she came full circle.

"Right," said the justice again.

Nakedness can be embarrassing.

"It was the bad company," the woman pushed.

"He's 24?" the justice asked.

"I swear if you give him another chance, you won't regret it. I'll see to that," she made a final desperate push. She meant it.

The justice began his speech.

"I always admire mothers, the way they stand up for their children," he paid her an awkward tribute. "This defendant has no previous convictions, the others have . . ." But, but, — it was an intolerable situation, black-guards and criminals besetting citizens. The son had had the gall to get into the witness box and spin a yarn . . . and, and, and — even if they had no previous convictions between them, he would feel justified in imposing the maximum sentence. Twelve months imprisonment each.

The woman, open-eyed, listened in horror. She leaned against the wall, moved slowly along the wall, opened the courtroom door, watched her son go down the stairs to the cells, stepped out of the courtroom, let the door swing closed behind her.

And then came the awful wail. The door opened and you could see her in the corridor, her head thrown back, wailing. It was a broad and jagged cry, unceasing, and you could hear it move, as she ran up and down, in and out of the building.

10 December 1975

The suspicious glazier

He had seen the defendant standing at a laneway, between two shops, in semi-darkness, the garda told District Justice Ó hUadhaigh in Dublin District Court 4. The garda thought he looked suspicious, and he told the defendant so and asked him for his name and address, which the defendant refused to give. He was in possession of a glass-cutter, and he told the garda that he was a glazier by occupation, but refused to give proof of this. The defendant's friend eventually arrived, but still the defendant refused to give his name and address and the garda "invited him up to the station," where, at 2.30 in the morning, he gave the required information.

"At that time," said the garda, "he wasn't to my knowledge a suspected person, but I have since discovered that he has one previous conviction for housebreaking."

The defendant cross-questioned the garda. "Did I give you proof of my identity?" he asked. The garda replied that he had offered a card with a name on it, but no photograph, except that of a girl. "And did you ask my friend for my name and did it correspond with the one on the card?" the defendant asked. The garda agreed, and added that he had advised the friend to advise the defendant to give his address, which he refused to do. The defendant was approximately six yards from the entrance of the pub at the laneway, in the semi-darkness, the garda said, and when asked why he was standing there, had replied that he was cold.

"Didn't I tell you I was only after coming out of a pub, and that if you'd hang on my mates would verify that?" asked the defendant. "Yes," said the garda. "Isn't that proof of what I was doing there?" the defendant asked the Justice. "You've made your point," the Justice replied.

"You can't break into a house with a glass-cutter. Didn't you say it was an offensive weapon?" the youth asked the garda. "I mentioned that it could be a house-breaking instrument and your friend agreed with me," the garda replied.

"He did not," said the youth. "You said it was an offensive weapon and dangerous, and could mark somebody, and I gave you a demonstration that it wasn't by rubbing it along my face, and there were no marks."

"You're entitled to a direction on the Vagrancy Act charge, because at the time when the guard approached you you weren't a suspected person," said the Justice. "So you're entitled to a dismissal, on the evidence, of the charge of loitering with intent to steal. Now there's possession of a housebreaking instrument." The Justice then invited the youth to give his story or say nothing at all, whichever he wished.

"I had the glass cutter in my pocket because I work at cutting glass," said the youth. "I brought it into work with me on Saturday morning, which I do every day, and I take it home with me."

"I asked you where you worked and you wouldn't tell me. Why?" asked the garda. "I was afraid you'd implicate me at my place of work. The boss doesn't like anything like that," the youth said. "I said I wouldn't tell your boss," said the garda. "I couldn't be sure of that," said the youth. "I said to you that I could prove to you that I was a glass-cutter. Now how could . . ."

"Dismiss," said the Justice.

24 July 1973

Epilogue
Into the Eighties

I

The man in the dock of Dublin Court 6 was well dressed, in a dark blue suit, with dark blue tie, and light blue shirt. His shoes were spiffily polished. The guard, in civilian clothes, took the witness stand. He told District Justice McCarthy that he had been walking along O'Connell Street the week before, off duty, on leave, in the company of a woman friend from down the country. They had been shopping. As they crossed O'Connell Bridge a bottle broke at his feet, which he picked up and put in the litter bin.

Three people approached them of whom the defendant was one, and begged from them. "I asked them to please let us pass by". About ten yards further on he was struck from behind, on the ear. He turned round and the defendant struck him with his fist. He held the defendant who then butted him with his head.

The defendant pleaded guilty to assault, obstructing and resisting arrest. He was not guilty of begging, he said. The guard testified that he had sent his woman friend to telephone the police. He remained on the bridge, holding the defendant, who resisted. The guard later went for X rays, and was still now suffering from twinges. There had been a swelling on his right cheek and soreness behind his right ear. He had been refused permission to leave the country, pending the court case, which he had to prosecute, he finished.

In answer to the female defence solicitor, the guard said that all three people on the bridge had some drink taken, and that this defendant was dressed differently a week ago than he was today. He had been wearing an open necked shirt then and a brown jacket. "I am used to seeing beggars on the street. He was actually begging", he rejected the solicitor's suggestion that her client had been doing no such thing.

"You will admit that he doesn't look like that sort of person", the solicitor persisted.

"That", said the guard, "is a matter of opinion. He had no collar or tie on . . ."

The defendant took the stand.

He had been going to catch the bus out to his sister's house, he said, when he saw two itinerants on the bridge, and the guard beside them, holding one by the arm and shouting at them. "I said to him 'Ah, let them go' and he grabbed me by the arm and said 'You'll do, I'll frame you'. Those were his exact words, your honour. I resisted, because he was in plain clothes, like, and he never showed me a cop card or anything".

He denied that he had been begging at any time.

The Justice convicted.

The man had nineteen convictions between 1966 and 1979, the guard said, his last being larceny in February 1979 for which he had received a twelve month prison sentence.

The guard went through the thirty-nine-year-old man's adult criminal career, starting with a fine for larceny in Brighton, in 1966; six weeks for assaulting the police in 1967; three months for larceny in Brighton, 1968; suspended driving licence for drunken driving in New Zealand, 1968; deported from New Zealand in 1969 for defecting from his ship; three jail terms in the seventies for assaulting his wife, who had got a separation order; nine months for larceny in April 1978; and twelve months for larceny in February 1979.

The defence solicitor said that her client had been working for his brother in England, since the beginning of 1980, as a builder's labourer. He had only recently returned to Ireland to apply to the High Court for access to his three children whom he had not seen for two years. He had a drink dependency and the guard had corroborated that drink played a part in the events of the week before. "He has pleaded guilty to the most serious charges here of assault, resistance and obstruction, but he is concerned that a begging charge should not appear on his record, for the sake of his family." Her client did not want his relatives to think that he was down and out.

"Convict of begging, one month", said the Justice. "On the other charges, convict, six months each, to run concurrently".

12 June 1980

II

There was a prohibition against selling flowers in the street off Grafton Street, in the manner in which the women had been selling them, the young guard told District Justice McGrath in Dublin District Court 6. As the result of a complaint he had gone to the street corner, cautioned them to move on, and had returned twenty-five minutes later to find them still there, still selling.

Two healthy and disgruntled young women, their cheeks red from the fresh air, stood impatiently in the dock.

"There were four Guinness barrels standing on the street and baskets or boxes of flowers laid out on top. On the other side of the street there were more Guinness barrels and more baskets of flowers stacked up on them. . . the position of the stalls was an obstruction to traffic, Justice", the guard gave his evidence.

"If you want to sell flowers there, it's not prohibited", one young woman put to him.

"I explained to them that street trading from baskets hung around the neck is allowed", the guard was stiff.

"We have a TD fighting our cause for us. He said he was

going to do something for us", the other young woman explained to the Justice.

"The reason for the complaints is that there are a number of flower shops in the area and they have to pay high rates and compete with these people" — the guard spilled the beans on his informers.

"Before any of those shops that sell flowers opened up, we were there before them. Everybody knows who I am", the first woman defended her proud city-centre tradition. "As regards the baskets sitting on the barrels, the guard was right about that", she defended her reluctant oppressor. "The TD says he'll look into it and the cops say they're willing to give us a licence", she finished, marshalling the forces of the state against the bourgeoisie.

"You remember I approached ye and explained about the baskets round your neck?", the prosecuting guard smilingly joined in her defence campaign.

"Yes, but you came back in five minutes after saying you'd be away for ten", she reminded him of how she had arrived at this sorry stage.

"And I escorted ye down to the station", he was hurt.

"Convict", the Justice intruded.

On the fifteenth of May, just four weeks earlier, Bridget had been fined £15 and Margaret had been similarly treated for the same sentence, the guard said. "The situation is that the law is as it is at the moment", the Justice told the young women. "You must comply with the law unless and until it is changed, regardless of whatever representation your TD is making". He fined them five pounds each, on each of three charges, with fourteen days to pay or seven days imprisonment in default.

No wonder "My Fair Lady" wasn't set in Ireland.

14 June 1980

III

A modest middle aged woman entered the witness box of Dublin District Court 6 to go bail for her son.

"What is your occupation?", the Justice asked her.

"Housewife", she named the condition that has been hymned in praise by Church and State.

Where would she get £100 if the defendant did not appear to answer charges, the Justice asked.

"I have me husband's wages. And then I do a bit of cleaning work meself", the woman said.

"How much do you earn a week?", the Justice asked.

"Twenty pounds", she replied.

"I can't accept you. I'm refusing you", the Justice rejected this mother, this cleaning woman, this wife. Her lifetime's work of rearing children and scrubbing office floors and keeping a marriage together was not sufficient to buy her son's freedom, while awaiting trial.

14 June 1980

Another Ward River Bestseller!

Val Dorgan
CHRISTY RING
A Personal Portrait

Fast-moving, frank, full of excitement and fresh revelations, this is a deeply personal portrait of Cork's greatest hurler. Val Dorgan, seasoned journalist and former Glen Rovers team-mate of Christy Ring, brings his own unique brand of insight and reminiscence to make a truly memorable tribute.

'The controversy about whether the book should be published at all or not, assures the publishers of a "best seller" on their hands, and once bought, the book makes compulsive reading. . . I found I could not leave it down. . . This book to me enhances Christy's reputation (if that is possible). . . the man emerges from the book with an abundance of fine qualities.'

EDDIE KEHER, Sunday Independent

A Paperback Original, illustrated

IR£3.30*
UK£3.00

ISBN 0 907085 06 7

* includes VAT

Another Ward River Bestseller!

Christina Murphy

SCHOOL REPORT

The Guide To Irish Education for Parents, Teachers and Students

Over the past ten years, Irish education has changed almost beyond recognition. Here at last, Christina Murphy of *The Irish Times* answers all the vital questions, explains the current situation and future trends, and provides sound advice on a host of topics including:

Which school? National or Private? Secondary, Vocational, Community? Who owns our schools? How can parents take part in school management? How does the 'points' system work? What is the New Curriculum? What about religion and sex education? Which careers are open to school leavers? And many other topics.

With 256 pages and 27 tables giving all the facts and figures, this is the most useful guide to the system ever published. If you have a child at school, then you need SCHOOL REPORT.

A Paperback Original
ISBN 0 907085 00 8
UK £2.00
IR £2.20 including VAT

'An invaluable resource book' Forum, RTE

Another Ward River Bestseller!

Pan Collins

IT STARTED ON THE LATE LATE SHOW

A Paperback Original

What lies behind the smooth professionalism of Gay Byrne's Late Late Show? Has it really changed Irish society? How is this fantastically successful TV show actually put together?

Pan Collins, senior researcher, tells the backroom story of the men and women behind the Late Late Show. How it began. The early years. What Gay Byrne is like to work with. The team. The recipe for success. What happens when an international star fails to turn up on the night.

The big names are all here: James Mason, Michael Mac Liammoir, Oliver Reed, Mary Whitehouse. So too are all the details of "specials" like the Toy Show, the "penguin" show and the 500th Late Late Show. But Ireland sees itself mirrored in the Late Late Show, and the most explosive audience reaction has come when the Show tackled such delicate issues as parapsychology, lesbianism and the taxation of farmers.

For wit, warmth and sheer readibility, Pan Collins has written the showbiz book of the decade.

ISBN 0 907085 00 8
IR£2.75*
UK£2.50

*includes VAT